A PARS

AND

HIS PARISH

The work of the Reverend George Arbuthnot
Vicar of Stratford-on-Avon 1879–1908

Freda Kitcher

GEM PUBLISHING COMPANY, WALLINGFORD

Gem Publishing Company
Brightwell cum Sotwell
Wallingford, Oxfordshire OX10 0QD

First published October 2006

British Library Cataloguing in Publication Data.
A catalogue record for this book is available from the British Library.

ISBN 0 906802 12 1

Designed and typeset in Bembo by
Gem Publishing Company, Wallingford, Oxfordshire.
Printed in England by Henry Ling Ltd, The Dorset Press, Dorchester.

For

Norman, John, David, Lilian and Jan

I wish to record my gratitude for the help and encouragement I have received from the late Dr Levi Fox, O.B.E. (former Director of the Shakespeare Birthplace Trust), Dr Robert Bearman and Mairi Macdonald (Head and Deputy Head of Archives at the Shakespeare Birthplace Trust respectively), Felicity Howlett, Norma Hampson, Margaret Pettifer, John Kitcher, Geoffrey Morton, Freda Morton, John Hill, Sue Hill and most of all, my dear husband, Norman Kitcher.

Front Cover: The north porch of Holy Trinity Church, Stratford-upon-Avon.
Back Cover: Holy Trinity Church, Stratford-upon-Avon.

Photograph: Felicity Howlett

The Reverend George Arbuthnot
(By permission of the Vicar of Holy Trinity Church, Stratford, The Revd Martin Gorick.)

CONTENTS

SOURCES

Apart from the footnotes, and the dates of the deaths of George and Margaret Arbuthnot, all information in this book has been gleaned from Holy Trinity Magazines published in Stratford-on-Avon between 1880 and 1908.

The magazine always names the town Stratford-on-Avon or Stratford. Today, officially, the town is called Stratford-upon-Avon while the district remains Stratford-on-Avon.

Please note, the use of capital letters in the magazines is both prolific and inconsistent.

PREFACE

The Reverend George Arbuthnot
Vicar of Stratford-on-Avon 1879–1908

George Arbuthnot came to Stratford from Arundel in West Sussex where he had served, firstly as curate, then as Vicar. He was aged thirty-three and he was unmarried.

Stratford was a small market town. The railways and the canals were working, but most travel was still by horse or on foot. Farmwork, shopwork and domestic service were the chief means of earning a living; all were poorly paid and entailed long hours. The most important industry was Flower's Brewery. Among certain families in the town there was real poverty. There was, of course, no National Health, no job security, no pensions and no dole.

The new Vicar had been educated at Eton and Christ Church, and he seems to have been influenced by the Oxford Movement. He was wealthy, having been left a great deal of money by his father. He bought 'The Firs', a substantial house with a large garden, which was situated where the police station now stands.

He had a strong social conscience which drove him tirelessly to improve conditions in the town. He had vision and zeal, and was able to gather a team of dedicated helpers.

Above all, he truly believed that 'all are equal in the sight of God, and that neither rank nor wealth should ever take precedence at the Lord's Table'.

Chapter 1

THE PARISH MAGAZINE

Within two months of coming to Stratford, The Reverend George Arbuthnot started a Parish Magazine. Most of the printed matter was published nationally. First, a publication called *Home Words* was chosen, followed by *The Banner of Faith*, but subsequently, for nineteen years, *The Church Monthly* was selected. These magazines contained highly moral stories, rather sentimental pictures, newly published hymns, and similar articles. Usually a description of a famous church was included and often a profile of a leading clergyman. The portrait of Henry Philpot, Bishop of Worcester, must have been of particular interest to the Parish since Stratford, at that time, was in his diocese. The Vicar wrote: 'A few years ago a Parish Magazine was a rare thing, now it is a recognised part of the machinery of every well-worked Parish. And not only this but it is also most useful – it serves as a means of communication between a Parish Priest and his people, it binds Parishioners together by making known to all common objects of interest, it promotes the observance of Church Seasons and Festivals by explaining their object.'

People were urged to buy two copies, one for themselves and one for their servants. It was also used as a method of keeping in touch with sons and daughters who had left Stratford. For a penny-halfpenny a month, Morgans, the printers, would post a copy to anywhere in Britain. For a further sum, one could be sent to anywhere in the world. By the end of 1881 a thousand copies were being printed every month. Morgan's also bound twelve monthly copies together, at a charge of one and sixpence, making a handsome volume.

An almanac was published each year, too. This was advertised in 1888:

Sheet Almanac

A Parish Almanac has been ordered, and will shortly be on sale by the District Visitors at three-half-pence. It is so cheap because we wish it to find a place in every house, but the cost involves a loss of over 12*s.*, so it is hoped that those who can afford it, will give twopence for it.

N.B. Don't hang it too high on your walls, as the local information is at the top.

D.V. The Vicar will preach on the illustrations next Lent.

The charge of one penny for each copy of the magazine did not cover the cost of production and local firms were asked to pay for advertising space.

These make interesting reading since they include many well-known Stratford businesses and, in some cases, examples of the goods they sold and the prices they charged. In some years a special Christmas Edition was also printed.

Over the years, in spite of its popularity, the Vicar continually pleaded for more advertisers. Publication often had to be subsidised by generous patrons. The pages of most interest are, of course, those at the back of each issue which dealt with local affairs. These, along with his pulpit, became Arbuthnot's platform from which he promoted his Parish work. He was not the editor, but it would be very surprising if any article was printed of which he disapproved. He wrote a monthly letter, and even when he was away on holiday, communications from as far away as Scandinavia, Italy and America were included. Regular services were printed on the annual almanac but each month all the additional special services were advertised. For Christmas and Easter the names of the preachers are given. Many visiting speakers were invited. Some of the sermons are printed in the magazine and others, which were printed separately, were advertised in it. From time to time the Vicar would explain the meaning of the teachings of the Church, like the importance of Holy Communion, the Creeds, or the Seasons of Lent. The Parish was made aware of the new legal requirements affecting the Church and its ministry. For example, the following passage appeared in 1901:

The Parish Clerk

> A change in the law, which came into force on January 1st, has stopped all payment of burial fees to the Parish Clerk, when the funeral takes place in the cemetery. Mr Bennett will in consequence not be expected to attend at the cemetery, unless his presence is especially desired by the mourners, in which case notice will have to be given at the time when the funeral arrangements are made, and the fee hitherto payable at the Town Clerk's office will have to be made to him.

Regular features were announcements of changes to the team of clergymen in the Parish, and the particular area in which each man would serve. Every issue contained a list of baptisms, marriages and burials which had taken place in the previous month. Appreciative obituaries were written about those who had served the Church in various capacities.

Financial statements were printed in great detail and also many, many lists of subscribers to the rebuilding funds, school funds, overseas missions, choir outings and a host of other activities. The smallest amount would be acknowledged – the Vicar was ever grateful for small contributions from people who could afford little – but financial statements were nearly always followed by an appeal for further funds.

The magazines sometimes contained advertisements for work: caretakers, vergers, and other servants of the Church. Applications were sought from those wishing to train as pupil teachers in the National School. A boy who wished to have a job as messenger boy for the Vicar was requested to apply at the Vicarage and 'must be a pupil at the National School, and must be sharp and thoroughly reliable'.

Another boy was required to look after the pony, work in the garden, live in the house and 'must be able to ride well'.

Lastly, the magazines advertised and reported all the Church activities: missions, concerts, Sunday School outings and Band Meetings – and it is these activities which give such a vivid picture of life in this Parish a hundred years ago.

Chapter 2

SERVICES

George Arbuthnot thought the whole arrangement of the Church buildings was important to worship. Seats should be positioned where clergy could be seen and heard. The building should be well lit. The correct liturgical colours should be used on the appropriate festivals, and clergy and choir should look smart in their robes. In addition, he desired a high standard of musicianship.

By 1889 he could write in the magazine:

> Everything in this Parish makes Church-going easy. The Services are bright and cheerful, and not too long. The seats are all free and unappropriated; the sermons are short and easy to be understood; the singing is congregational and hearty.

In 1880, at Holy Trinity, and at St James', Holy Communion was celebrated at 8 a.m., Morning Prayer was at 11 a.m. and Evensong at 7 p.m. At Holy Trinity a Children's Service was held in the afternoon. Shottery had services at 11 a.m. and 7 p.m., and Luddington had a service at 3.30 p.m. There was an extra communion service at each Church on one Sunday in each month. On weekdays Holy Trinity had early Matins at 10.15 a.m. and Choral Evensong at 5 p.m. St James' had daily Matins at 8 a.m. and Evensong at 7.30 p.m. This service never lasted longer than a quarter of an hour and the Vicar urged 'poorer brethren' to attend. 'It is a wonderful help to go and spend a few quiet moments in God's House,' he wrote. He also urged the congregation to attend in their working clothes.

Gradually more Communion Services were introduced until by 1908 a daily Celebration was held at Holy Trinity.

There were also many week-night services, classes and study groups.

Very special preparations were made for the seasons of Lent and Advent, followed by the celebrations of Easter and Christmas. Each Spring and Autumn the Vicar's letter would include a paragraph on the virtue of self-denial followed by a timetable of talks and sermons for the weeks before each Festival.

The Great Feast Days of Whitsun, Ascension Day, and many Saints' Days were marked by special services with visiting preachers, anthems and, often, processions. St James' Day became a particularly important celebration with a Garden Party on the Vicarage Lawn, as well as Church Services. Shakespeare's Birthday Ceremonies grew in importance at this time.

Many special occasions were marked – openings of restored buildings, the unveiling of new windows, concerts given on restored organs – each with special prayers and invited guests.

Events of national importance were celebrated, including Queen Victoria's

Golden and Diamond Jubilees, King Edward VII's Coronation, and the ending of the Boer War. There were also special services for such domestic issues as Home Missions, the Curates' Fund and Local Hospitals. Several times during these years Missions were held when a team of visiting clergy made special efforts to inspire the Congregation to deeper faith.

Arbuthnot firmly believed that the Celebration of Holy Communion is the chief act of Christian Worship. He never failed to exhort his congregation to take part as often as possible. Attendance at an early service was advisable, preferably before breakfast, but those that came at mid-day 'did not err'. He had stern words for those who came later. In a sermon, quoted in a magazine, he spoke of those 'who put attendance at the Lord's Supper on the same level as a dinner party or a concert, and think that having given the day to themselves, they may offer the evening to God. I feel that in the very vast majority of cases, such a practice is absolutely sinful.'

The Vicar was deeply upset on the occasion when a Celebration could not take place because no-one was present to partake. He finally got permission to hold the daily service for even one communicant.

He used many methods to increase the number. All newly confirmed youngsters were encouraged to make a habit of attending regularly, instead of making a first communion and falling away. The members of the Guild of the Holy Cross and the Guild of the Daughters of the Church attended regular services.

On certain Feast Days an early celebration was held at 5 a.m. for those who had to be at work by 6 a.m.

It was a cause for great rejoicing in 1904 when 1,040 communicants went up to the Parish Altars on Easter Day.

As usual, much advice was given. People were urged not to be in too big of a hurry to reach the altar rail. Too long a wait could diminish reverence and devotion. They were advised to study their prayer books or suitable hymns. Recipients were advised to sip a larger quantity of wine. He felt that some did no more than put their lips to the chalice. Above all, the congregation was reminded that everyone was EQUALLY welcome at the LORD'S TABLE and that the rich should never expect to take precedence over the poor.

A firm believer in the sanctity of marriage, the Vicar did not approve of divorce. He wrote:

> I must refuse the use of the Church for any marriage, in which one of the parties has a husband or wife living, from whom the civil law may have divorced them. The Church does not recognise divorce, or any severance of the bond 'until death'.

He also took the ruling of the Prayer Book very seriously. In 1896 he reported that a colleague had found out, by the merest chance, that one couple, whose bans had been asked, and no hindrance had been alleged, were within the prohibited degrees of relationship. The clergyman had refused to perform the ceremony, but another clergyman in a neighbouring parish obliged. This did not set a good example, he wrote, and neither money nor aristocratic connections could make it right.

Nor did George Arbuthnot approve of weddings in Registry Offices. In 1902 he wrote:

> I feel I must repeat the warning I have given before, that for Church people to contract a union before the Registrar, instead of in Church, is to overlook the sacred character of the marriage bond, and to forfeit the blessing of God upon the union. The only marriages which ought to be performed before the civil official, in the quiet of the Registry Office, are those in which their conscience tells the man and the woman that they have no right to come to Church for the ceremony, or where the Church does not recognise the lawfulness of the union. In the former case I must repeat the notice I have given before, that I feel obliged to decline to Church the woman after the birth of her first child.

The Vicar liked to conduct all Marriage Services at the Parish Church personally. The usual hours were 8.30 a.m., 9.45 a.m. or 10.30 a.m. on any day except Sunday. Other times could be specially arranged. Weddings were not encouraged during Lent. Prince Leopold, it was said, set a good example to all bridegrooms by postponing his marriage until after Easter.

Bans for Church Weddings were read out, of course, but were not published in the magazine. During the latter years of the Vicar's incumbency, the 'purposes of marriage' notices for couples living in the Parish were printed along with the name of the chapel where the ceremony would take place and sometimes stating 'without any religious service'.

Many Baptisms took place on Wednesdays at the Parish Church at 5 p.m. and at St James' at 7 p.m. Sundays were preferred, and a card was given to any infant christened that day. Services were held at 2.30 p.m. at Holy Trinity, and at 7 p.m. at St James' and St Andrew's.

So many were christened with the name of William, that a list of suggested boys' names was published together with their meanings. This was followed by a similar list for girls. A good many addresses were devoted to reminding parents of their obligations to their offspring, and to children, showing their duty to their parents.

More advice was given about funerals and burials by the Vicar. His arrival in 1879 coincided with the proposal to close the churchyard for burials and to open the new cemetery in the Evesham Road. He took the opportunity to remind his parishioners that the freehold of the churchyard was invested in the incumbent. He therefore felt justified in asking for certain standards in the choice of gravestones which should have simple brief inscriptions such as 'In Peace', or 'Here rests in God', along with the name and date of the deceased. He also requested that those who planted flowers and shrubs on graves should undertake to maintain them.

In 1880 the Bishop of Worcester consecrated part of the new area. Arbuthnot was much concerned that those who had been regular worshippers in his Church should be interred in that section, and that Holy Trinity, St James' or St Andrew's, Shottery, should be the setting for the first part of the service, rather than the unconsecrated chapel which had been built at the cemetery – though as priest, he would officiate at the funeral of any parishioner in either area. He also wished the

Church bell to be tolled instead of the one in the new chapel.* Ever practical, he reminded the mourners that the fee was the same whichever bell was used. In 1882 he wrote:

> It grieves me not to hear our Bell as heretofore, when the solemn procession moves up our Church Avenue. That Bell has called the congregation to Church when many of you were baptised, it has rung for your confirmation, and perhaps for your wedding, surely you must also wish it to be tolled when you are brought to Church for the last time.

He also observed that it was more widely heard in the town.

The distance to the new cemetery was about three-quarters of a mile and this posed further problems. Everyone, of course, was used to walking, but some families liked to hire a horse-drawn hearse. The Vicar was not happy with this. He published the following statement:

> It has hitherto been the custom for the clergyman who reads the funeral service in Church, to walk in his surplice, at the head of the procession, to the Cemetery. It is felt, however, that this is inconvenient, and even ridiculous, in the case of a driving funeral, so that in future, when a hearse or carriage is used, the clergyman will take off his robes, and walk by himself to the Cemetery, and meet the funeral party there. A very nice hand bier and pall are kept at the Church, and let out with bearers on extremely moderate terms, and when this is used the procession of the priest and mourners is most seemly, and will be maintained as hitherto.
>
> We are sorry to learn that the use of the bier is not universal. We commend it to all our readers as greatly preferable to any conveyance by horses.

Some criticism had been made that clergy and mourners were leaving the graveside before the coffin was covered by earth. It was agreed that the clergyman performing the funeral would remain until the mourning party retired. The Vicar hoped that this would be regarded as a mark of respectful sympathy. The filling of the grave, or not, immediately after the service, was optional.

Further advice was necessary about the times of funerals. This notice is typical:

> **FUNERALS**
>
> The Vicar wishes to request all Parishioners to be kind enough to consult him before fixing the hour of a funeral. While he is anxious at all times to suit the convenience of mourners, he begs to remind them that a funeral in the middle of the afternoon takes one of the clergy from his work among the living, and spoils the best part of the day. As a rule during the summer months, the most convenient hour is half-past five, directly after Evensong; but when that is impossible, twelve o'clock or two o'clock can be named. But it is always best to go to the Vicarage, before going to the Town Clerk's Office.

Four o'clock was a favourite time in winter.

A Choral funeral Service was highly recommended, on the following conditions:

---

* The bell from the Cemetery Chapel was moved to Holy Trinity Church in 1994, where it is used as a service and Sanctus bell.

1. the deceased, if confirmed, must have been a communicant;
2. the funeral must be a walking one – no hearse, and certainly no shillibeer★ being used;
3. there is a small extra charge of 2/6*d*. but this is willingly paid for by the Vicar in the case of poor persons;
4. the Processional Cross can be used, or not, at the wish of the mourners.

Arbuthnot showed his usual concern for the poor members of his congregation by publishing a table of expenses for funerals. The average price of a good coffin was £1.5*s*.0*d*. (£1.25). The hire of the Church bier WITH the pall and two men to wheel it was 3/- (15p) and a charge for a grave where the site was allocated was 12/- (60p), amounting to a total of £2.0*s*.0*d*. The men wheeling the bier were not to be given extra money. He hoped these guide-lines would help Parishioners at what is always a 'sorrowful and perplexing time'. If the bier was hired WITHOUT the pall, an extra 7/6*d*. (37.5p) was charged. This was because families covered the coffin with expensive wreaths instead of one simple floral tribute, so the Vicar reasoned that they could afford to pay more.

Arbuthnot did his best to transfer his ideas of simple memorials to the new cemetery. He was able to charge £5 for a memorial to be put on a grave, but he was prepared to return £4 of the fee upon three conditions:

1. the monument was in the form of a cross;
2. the inscription was submitted to him before it was cut, and was not to include any doggerel verse;
3. friends must promise that no imitation flowers or glass shades would be placed on the grave, either after the funeral, or at any time in the future.

The promise referred to in rule 3 was asked for in writing.

Burial services were carried out with great dignity. Any child of the Sunday School or choir who died aroused particular compassion.

When a congregation misbehaved, however, the Vicar could be very forthright. On one occasion some men arrived drunk at a funeral service. A warning was given that should it happen again, the constable would be sent for and the culprits taken into custody.

The burial of suicides caused the Vicar much disquiet. After several unhappy cases in 1903 he referred the matter to the Bishop who gave instruction that in all cases only an abbreviated form of Service could be used and that the body could not be taken into the Church. In the same year he wished to extend the area of consecrated ground at the cemetery since the Church area was getting overcrowded. The solution of cremation was raised. His comment was, 'There is nothing distinctly anti-Christian in the cremation of those remains . . . but on the other hand there is clearly no support in Holy Scripture for the practice.' He added, 'I greatly doubt if it will ever become very general.'

In 1880, at the beginning of his incumbency, Arbuthnot made a curious reference to the 'wake' when preaching at Shottery. He expressed a hope that no attempt would be made to revive it.

★ A shillibeer was a horse-drawn hearse promoted by George Shillibeer, pioneer of London Omnibuses.

George Arbuthnot was indefatigable in his efforts to make worship accessible to the whole Parish. No detail of Church practice was too insignificant to receive instruction – the importance of kneeling at prayer, the moment to stand before a hymn, or the inclination of the head towards the Altar during the Creed.

He ran many classes on sections of the Scriptures and printed articles on the meaning of the Great Feasts, the Sacraments and the Creeds. He also explained several controversial issues like the doctrine of the 'Real Presence', the place of Confession in the Church of England and the importance of the Apostolic Succession.

He was eager that his Congregation should have the opportunity of hearing some of the foremost preachers of the day and many of their sermons as well as some of his own and his curates were made available in print, either in the magazines or in pamphlet form. Sometimes part of a sermon was even published in the local newspaper.

It was an age of 'sermon tasting'; text, content and delivery would be keenly discussed over lunch and supper. I have been told that there were queues outside Holy Trinity before Evensong. Most of the Congregation would have a good knowledge of the Scriptures and would be quick to pick up any reference. In Stratford, it would seem, they were expected to be familiar with the works of Shakespeare, too.

The themes of sermons were often announced in advance and distinguished preachers were given 'star billing'. In 1884 The Choral Association of the Archdeaconry of Coventry held a Music Festival at Holy Trinity on Tuesday, July 8th at 3 pm. The preacher was to be 'the celebrated Canon Knox-Little, by many considered the most eloquent man in the Church of England'. The congregation was advised to be early.

Chapter 3

THE CLERGY AND OTHER CHURCH STAFF

When George Arbuthnot came to Stratford, the Parish was in the hands of the Rev. Frank Smith*, the Priest Chaplain, who had a special responsibility for the Workhouse. He was a popular, jovial Irishman who became a much valued partner in the Parish for the next twenty years. The Rev. G. F. Grundy had been appointed to take the sole charge of St James' Church and, disliking the new Vicar's system of a 'team' ministry, he resigned 'after twelve months' friendly connection to our no less friendly separation'. A third clergyman, the Rev. J. F. C. Williams, had temporarily helped the Parish during the interregnum. He left in February 1880 and the Rev. V. K. Fortescue joined the staff. The Fortescue family lived at Alvescot Manor and the curate lived at the Lodge. From that date, Arbuthnot endeavoured to keep a staff of at least four men. He pointed out that, with the help of the Priest Chaplain, all the legal obligations of the Church to the Parish could be fulfilled, but officiating at baptisms, weddings and funerals, and preparing candidates for confirmation, was not enough; he believed that his growing Parish needed a strong, active team, prepared to work for social reform as well as taking services.

Before he left Stratford in 1908, over twenty assistants came to work with him. Frank Smith was an older man, and Grundy was twelve years his senior, but mostly the new men were young and for many of them it would have been a first appointment. It was apparent that he was able to attract hard-working, able men, though few stayed for long because each one was hoping to gain a Parish of his own.

The Vicar's biggest problem was finding the means by which to pay the curates. Every year he paid part of their salaries out of his own pocket, and certain expenses, which he could have claimed for himself, went into the 'Curates Fund'. Once or twice he was able to have five staff, but he was sometimes reduced to three when he could not afford the extra money. A few of the men were married and their wives gave much service within the Parish, too.

The workload was heavy. Sunday and weekday services had to be arranged at four Churches, but that was only part of the work. In 1901 he wrote:

> It is sometimes said that Sunday is 'our busy day'; I prefer to put it that we are busy *every day*, and in order to prove this I ask you to consider the correspondence

---

* Frank Smith was so well liked that, when he died several years after leaving the Parish, the beautiful cross on the High Altar in Holy Trinity was given in his memory.

and arrangements which are involved in the work of a Parish of nearly 10,000 people, and Schools of nearly 1,000 children; of the Classes and Meetings held on week-days; and also to notice the returns which I am able to give of pastoral visits paid during the year.

I have entries of 5775 visits paid by myself and my Colleagues, giving an average of 111 a week. Of these about 900 have been paid to those in sickness, in addition to the cases I have already referred to, when the Holy Communion was administered.

Another aspect of our work is in connection with the Schools. The Sunday Schools are under the direct management of the Clergy, and I never fail to visit them myself when at home. But besides this it is our privilege to take part in the religious instruction in the Day School, and although I do not suggest that our teaching is equal to that of the regular staff, I think the knowledge thus gained of the children is very useful to us, and I hope our presence is encouraging to the teachers.

To show the number of hours worked by the clergy on Easter Day 1897, he published the following table:

It may interest our Readers to know the hours which the Clergy of the Parish spent in Church on Easter Day, so we give them below:

The Vicar, 6.30 to 9.30 a.m., 11 a.m. to 1.30 p.m., 2.45 to 4 p.m., 7 to 8.30 p.m.; $8\frac{1}{4}$ hours.

The Priest-Chaplain, 6.30 to 9.00 a.m., 11 a.m. to 1.30 p.m., 7 to 8.30 p.m.; $6\frac{1}{2}$ hours.

Rev. H. Wilson, 6.30 to 9.45 a.m., 11 to 1.30 p.m. 7 to 8.30 p.m.; $7\frac{1}{4}$ hours.

Rev. W.C. Allsebrook, same as the Vicar; $8\frac{1}{4}$ hours.

Rev. W.T.E. Carey, 7 to 8.15 a.m., 8.30 to 9.15 a.m., 11 to 1.15 p.m., 3.30 to 4.45 p.m., 7 to 8.30 p.m.; 7 hours.

Average nearly $7\frac{1}{2}$ hours each. Besides this, Mr Smith served the Workhouse twice; Mr H. Wilson, Bishopton Church, once; Mr Carey travelled 8 miles; and the Vicar and Mr Allsebrook were in Sunday School for nearly an hour.

The following month another paragraph was inserted:

Some have noticed the paragraph in our last, and say that no account should be taken of it, because it tells of an exceptional day. We give the working hours of one of the Clergy of the Parish on an ordinary Sunday – *ex uno disce omnes*. Start for Church 7.45. In Church 7.55 to 8.50. Home to breakfast at 9. Start for Sunday School 9.35. In Sunday School 9.45 to 10.35. To Church, In Church 11–12.40. Home to dinner at 1. Start for Church 2.30. In Church 2.45 to 4. Home to tea and rest. Start for Church 6.45. In Church 7 to 8.30. Home to supper and bed.

Much help with what we would now call 'youth work' was expected, including outdoor activities – football, rounders and cricket – in the Vicar's field. Temperance work also took up a great deal of time. Appointees did not have to sign the pledge but they were certainly expected to show an example by drinking only moderately. Arbuthnot was proud that W. T. E. Carey, who became the Organising Secretary for the Church of England Temperance Society for the Diocese of Ripon, had become an abstainer when he was Curate at Shottery. Unless there was a good reason, clergy were expected to be involved in all

Excursions and Treats for Sunday Schools, Day Schools, Band of Hope, Church Lads Brigade, Temperance Societies and Choirs. These were busy days acting as couriers, marshalls, games organizers and disciplinarians. They also produced concerts and readings, plays and social evenings. Each of the 'team' was allocated an area of the town with the Vicar having overall supervision. Within his 'patch' a curate was expected to visit every household at least twice a year. Non-church-going church people and dissenters were, nevertheless, Parishioners and must be included. One of the Vicar's favourite sayings was, 'House-going parsons make church-going people!'

The areas were roughly:

1. the North side of the line made by Bridge Street, Wood Street and Greenhill Street;
2. the area to the West of Rother Street and including Shottery and Luddington;
3. all the Old Town College Street area down to the railway and the river;
4. half the main area of the town divided by Church Street, Chapel Street and High Street;
5. the rest of the main area with Waterside and Southern Lane and the houses in Bridgetown.

These were altered from time to time according to the number of clergy working in the Parish. The clergy were not always welcome, as the following letter shows, but from the great number of visits made it would seem that they were generally well received.

VISITING

To the Parishioners.

My Dear Friends,

I wish to send you a short message through the Magazine on the subject of pastoral visitations. I conceive it to be the duty and the privilege of the Clergyman of any Parish to visit his Parishioners, quite apart from any visits he may pay them in sickness. He thus becomes acquainted with them, and better able to advise them in difficulty, and comfort them in trouble.

But with a Parish of this size, it is impossible for one man to become acquainted with everyone. The head of a Parish has a great many duties to perform which do not appear upon the surface, and I must depute some of my work to my Assistants. I have therefore divided the Parish into districts, in charge of each of which I have placed one of my Assistant Curates. It is his duty to visit, and to try to become personally acquainted with its residents, and he reports to me every week the results of his visits, and consults me on any doubtful question which may arise. Now the object of this letter is to ask for a kind and friendly reception for these Clergymen when they call. I am pained by hearing sometimes of people, when they hear their knock, coming to the window and looking out, and then paying no further attention. Now of course any householder is at liberty to decline a Clergyman's visit, but common courtesy would suggest that the door should be opened, and the fact that the person is engaged or would rather not be called upon, stated. A visit is intended as an act of friendship and politeness, and it should be accepted or declined as such.

I have asked my Clergy never to enter a house without first asking permission, 'May I come in'; but I have been obliged to add that when they are treated in the rude manner described, I think they are justified in passing over that house the next time they are calling in the street. I must not conclude this letter without stating that the vast majority of my Parishioners have always received me, and I think my Assistant Clergy too, in the most kind and friendly manner.

I remain, dear Friends,

Yours very faithfully,

G. Arbuthnot.

The Clergy lived at various addresses in the town. Church Street and College Street were popular.

In spite of all their hard work, the Clergy seem to have had a pleasant social life. We hear of outings where 'even the Vicar relaxed a little, while his colleagues wisely left their dignity at home'.

A sly reference was made to Mr Fortescue's courtship: 'While other clergy were engaged in athletic pastimes on an outing it was noted that Mr Fortescue "went for a walk among the trees with somebody".'

Poor Mr Newling failed to arrive at the Harvest Festival at St James' on time. His absence was 'caused by insufficient knowledge of the rather perplexing, though useful, little book commonly called Bradshaw'.

In 1904 when George Arbuthnot had completed twenty-five years as Vicar of Stratford, celebrations were arranged and many former Curates were invited back. From the accounts of this reunion we learn much about their subsequent careers. Frank Smith, the Priest Chaplain, a man of unfailing good humour, had been the longest serving member of the group. When he retired from Stratford he went to be Rector of Atherstone. His eldest son, J. J. Smith, also served as curate here for a time. He later became a Naval Chaplain serving on H.M.S. Curacao. He wrote to Arbuthnot when the ship visited Zanzibar where certain Missionary Work was supported by this Parish.

Another close friend was the Rev. G. H. Moor who served with Arbuthnot in Arundel for four years and joined him in Stratford for a further six years. He had the position of Precentor at Holy Trinity. The curate appointed to this position was obviously involved with the organist and the choir. Holy Trinity was a large and difficult Church to fill with sound, particularly in the first part of Arbuthnot's ministry when the Choir was placed under the crossover. The Precentor was frequently asked to organize fund-raising concerts, and he was much in demand as a soloist on many social occasions. When Rev. G. H. Moor left in 1884 it was partly because his voice was failing. He eventually became Vicar of Christ Church, Brighton. For a few years, his brother, the Rev. H. F. Moor, also served here. He left to go to Southampton in 1888 and died just eight weeks after his wedding. Stratford mourned him sincerely.

There is a hint that certain curates left when livings became vacant. One went when his father died. W. E. Newling, who 'became Vicar of Midsomer Norton, was begged by former friends to return to Bath'.

Several went to Parishes fairly near to Stratford, such as Inkpen, Aspull, Twycross, Bubbenhall and Badsey. Some moved further away, like H. Pentin, who went to Milton Abbey, and W. F. Aston, who went to Lee-on-Solent.

One or two had personalities which sparkle over the years. R. S. Genge* who became Vicar of Christ Church, Wolverhampton, seems to have been 'the life and soul of the party'. At the Choir Boys Christmas Entertainment, reported in 1890, 'Sir Gilbert Sullivan O'Genge – nearly related to one of our clergy, sang'. The Rev. A. F. Newton also took part in the concert.

R.S. Genge took rooms in the same house, 19 Church Street, as Newton. This circumstance has called forth the following touching lines:

The (Assistant) Curate's Dream

Ah me! ah you! Ah Everyone!
And, ah that blessed dream!
Ah, too, that line of Longfellows:
'Things are not what they seem.'

'I dreamt I dwelt in marble halls,'
Sang one, but in my dream
I'd found a lodging for myself
At Stratford-by-the-Stream.

And there I lived a Curate's life
In quite submissive way,
And smiled and groaned, preached and intoned
For very little pay.

And with me lived a brother man,
A curate like myself,
Who – just like me – on quarter day
Received but scanty pelf.

So as we both were getting thin
(Remember, 'twas a dream)
We hit upon a little plan
To help our need extreme.

Outside our door we hung a bask-
Et, hung it by a string,
That, as the faithful passed it by
Into it they might fling

Asparagus and broccolo
And cabbages galore,
And hares and rabbits, ribs of beef
To help keep wolf from door.

---

* Each year the Genge Bequest Award is given to a treble who has served the choir loyally, and has reached the end of his or her service.

Sea-kale in season – oh and once,
When I had friends to stay,
A lady dropped six peaches in –
They ate them all that day.

The Vicar, too, oftimes would go
Somewhere his health to harden,
And whilst away would send us veg-
Etables from his garden.

Till, gradually, our weight increased
As still our lot grew lighter,
Our generous friends, contented, said,
'Your cassocks, sir, grow tighter.'

Ah me! ah you! Ah everyone!
'Things are not what they seem,'
Longfellow said. I echo it!
'Twas but a blessed dream!

RSG

Newton became Rector of Maraisburg, South Africa.

Another man who went to serve in the Mission Field was the Rev J. Beck. At a Sunday School Treat at Kenilworth 'he attested his youthfulness by rushing wildly about clothed in a pink garment, laden with bags of sweets, and hotly pursued by a crowd of youngsters'. On a Band of Hope outing on the Avon, he reached out to help another boat and fell in. By 1904 he had left India and was Chaplain at Aden. The Rev. C. Price also went to India, and the Rev. H. J. Gully, whose health could no longer stand the damp climate of Stratford, found warmth at Buenos Aires.

The last four could not, of course, be present at the reunion, but a party of twenty-four sat down to dinner with the Arbuthnots on July 4th 1904.

At the end of the meal, 'the Rev. F. Smith, in the name of his brethren, presented the Vicar with a beautiful silver inkstand, and an address, as follows':

Dear Vicar,

When we received your kind invitation to commemorate on this day your twenty-five years Ministry in Stratford-upon-Avon, we felt that we ought not to allow this interesting re-union to take place without giving you some slight token of our regard and esteem. We thought it could not take a better form than an inkstand for use in the study where we had so many pleasant and helpful meetings in past years.

Of course we had at times different views as regards the manner in which we should discharge our important parochial duties; but I believe, must all gratefully remember your kindness and consideration for your fellow workers, as well as your helpful guidance, when presiding over our meetings.

I feel sure that we all agree that the discussions we have had in your study – opened always with prayer – were not only helpful when we were working in this

Parish but also have left with us many valuable lessons, which have been useful to us in other fields of labour.

We hope that you will kindly accept the gift we now present to you.

– Gerald Moor, H. Pentin, R. S. Genge, W. C. Allsebrook, W. E. Newling, V. Fortescue, T. Maude, T. J. Taylor, W. F. Aston, W. T. E. Carey, A. H. Parnell, G. F. Grundy, H. Wilson, R. G. K. F. Philpott, H. W. L. Ward, R. A. Norris, C. E. Bickmore, H. D. Butler, J. J. Smith, F. Smith.

Each of the clergy was allocated a vacation period every year, and sometimes we are told where they went. Occasionally one would take charge of another Church for a week or so – in England or abroad – and thus have 'a working holiday'. The Rev. H. Wilson took over a Parish in Cheshire, while R. A. Norris acted as Chaplain at Montana in Switzerland for four weeks. C. E. Bickmore went for a cycling holiday in Scotland in 1904 and had a very severe accident. While he was incapacitated, the Rev. Norris caught scarlet fever. So the Vicar had great problems covering the work of the Parish in the following months.

Apart from curates appointed to the Parish, many guests came to preach and lecture. Two clergymen who were often asked were the Chaplain at Trinity College, and the Incumbent of Bishopton – an appointment which was in the Vicar's gift. Headmasters of the Grammar School were also called upon to speak. Vicars of local churches were invited to special services – those from Loxley, Leamington, Wilmcote, Atherstone-on-Stour, Emscote, Snitterfield, Aston Cantlow, Hampton Lucy, Alveston and Clifford Chambers among them. Not all guest speakers were local clergymen. In 1884 those giving talks during Lent included the Archdeacon and the Dean of Worcester, Canon Butler of Worcester, the Vicar of St Michael's, Coventry, and the Assistant Curate of St Alban's, Birmingham.

The Luckock Family, George Arbuthnot's in-laws were always very supportive, and many special preachers came from the Home Missions, Overseas Missions, and the Temperance Movement.

Added to all of these, there were many distinguished prelates who graced the pulpit at the major Festivals and on the Shakespeare's Birthday Services. Thus the Parishioners of Stratford had access to a very wide variety of speakers including some who were regarded as the best of their age.

At all four Churches there were certain other paid appointments. The organists got the highest salaries. By 1907, £95 a year was paid at Holy Trinity, £25 at St James', £11 5*s.* 0*d.* at Shottery and £10 at Luddington. An organ blower and the choirboys were also paid. Bell ringers collected 'Christmas Boxes'. Clerks, Vergers, Sextons and, at Holy Trinity, Curators also received remuneration. Some of these posts were doubled up.

In 1896 the office of Verger at Holy Trinity was advertised. A new man was to be appointed because the former holder of the office was detected stealing money from one of the Church boxes and was therefore instantly dismissed. He was not prosecuted in consideration that he had a wife and young family, though he was named and, of course, everyone in the town must have known his identity. The duties were 'to attend all services on Sundays and any evening services during the week, i.e. Wednesdays and Saints' Days, lighting the gas, etc.' The salary was £10 per annum, and a uniform was given as required. During the winter months he was to stoke the fire for a further 4/- per week. £22 each year was allowed by the Churchwardens to provide for the cleaning of the Church and the washing of the surplices and linen. He could earn about £10 more by giving assistance to the Custodians in the busy season.

A year later the post of Verger at St James' was advertised. 'Applicants, who must be communicants, are invited to apply at once to the Vicar. The duties will include cleaning the Church, and the salary is £22 per annum. An abstainer will be preferred, but this is not absolutely necessary, though strict temperance is.'

Several of these men served the Churches for long periods of time. Mr Heeley retired, due to failure of health, in 1894, having been Clerk and Verger of St James' since it opened, and William Tysoe was Clerk and Sexton at Luddington for many years. Mr Wells, who served as Verger at Holy Trinity for twenty-three years, was presented with a testimonial and a purse of sovereigns. George Shirley was Verger and caretaker at Shottery for thirty years, and William Butcher was Clerk at Holy Trinity for a remarkable thirty-five years – and he was also the oldest member of the choir.

One other post was advertised. In 1899 a bicycle stand was provided for visitors, and an attendant could earn between 2/- and 6/- per week in the summer. Only boys who had been educated at the National School could apply.

Added to these was a host of voluntary workers in the Parishes. Headed by the Churchwardens there were Sidesmen, Choirmen, Servers at the Altar, Sunday School Teachers, Conductors of Classes, Conductors of Mothers' Union, Leaders of the Girls' Friendly Society, Members of the Guild of Church Decorators, Librarians, Secretaries of Missions and District Visitors.

The Wardens, Sidesmen and Synodsmen were elected or chosen at the Easter Vestry Meetings at Holy Trinity, St James' and Luddington. Shottery did not have a Vestry Meeting. Usually they were not well attended. 'Indeed,' said the Vicar, 'Vestry Meetings seldom are, unless a row is expected. They are useful safety valves to allow Parishioners to let off steam without bursting, but otherwise, since Church Rates have been abolished, they are of little practical use.'

However, the 1880 Meeting – the first meeting under the chairmanship of Arbuthnot – did not run smoothly. Three Wardens were accepted without opposition, but two men were nominated for the fourth position – Mr Pearce, the retiring Warden, and Mr Deer. A show of hands gave the post to Mr Deer, but Mr Pearce's supporters demanded a poll. This took place a week later, and Mr Pearce was returned by a good majority, probably because he supported the abolition of seat rents. It was thought that this was the first poll for a Churchwarden ever to have taken place in Stratford. The following years were mostly uneventful, and the Vicar expressed his opinion that it meant that people were content.

The Vicar tried to increase the number of men willing to serve by 'retiring' three out of six Sidesmen each year, but it had little effect as the same names recurred over and over again as Wardens, Sidesmen and representatives to Ruridecanal and Diocesan Meetings.

In 1886 further schemes to involve more Parishioners were promoted. A Parochial Council was formed. The Clergy and Wardens were to be ex officio members along with twenty-two members representing different interests of the

Parish. For example, the choirs of Holy Trinity and St James', the Ringers, the Sunday School Teachers, the Committee of the Church of England Temperance Society and the Vicar's Bible Class, could elect two representatives each.

The council was to meet quarterly and its function was to be consultative and advisory.

Members were asked to contribute any sum, not less than sixpence, towards expenses.

Matters like the need for a recreation ground in the town, the Education Bill of 1902, and Men's Services and Classes were discussed, but mostly little interest appears to have been shown, and often the quarterly meetings were not mentioned in the magazine. It was reported that at the October Meeting in 1903 'attendance was smaller than usual owing to the counter-attraction of the Mayor's Ball which proved to be too strong for the junior Clergy and about half the members'!

Chapter 4

PEW RENTALS

At Holy Trinity, as in many Anglican churches, the system of Pew Rentals was still in use. Wealthy families paid a sum to the Church in order to appropriate certain seats, or whole pews. These were reserved for their exclusive use, even if they were not attending the service. Poor people who dared to sit in a reserved seat were turned out either by a warden, or the lessee, when he arrived for a service.

George Arbuthnot was opposed to the practice, and wished to abolish it. In April 1880 he set out his reasons in the Parish Magazine.

> Appropriation encourages distinction of classes in Church, inasmuch as it is impossible to appropriate seats for everyone, and consequently they are assigned to the rich and not to the poor. But in the sight of both God and man all are equal and have equal rights in that Holy place. The law gives every parishioner who pays his rates, be he rich or poor, a vote on all subjects discussed at a Vestry Meeting, and thereby asserts the absolute equality of all. Appropriation also minimises the accommodation of a church, inasmuch as pews are appropriated to families, all of whose members are never present at one time, and even if they were, are not sufficiently numerous to fill the pew. Appropriation even breeds ill-will amongst those who have pews assigned to them, because all cannot possibly be equally well placed for taking part in the services. And appropriation, if fully carried out that is to say annually revised, causes infinite trouble to Churchwardens. For these and many other reasons I earnestly desire to see our Church freed from such evil.

His ideas received a mixed reception. One Churchwarden disagreed. Some parishioners were willing to give up their seats, others, having established themselves on the social ladder, were unwilling to forego their privileges. Some, indeed, claimed that they had given donations to a previous building programme on condition that certain seats could be rented. The situation at St James' Church was not so complicated. There had been no regular assignment of seats, though some pew rents were paid. These, the Vicar declined, and all seats were made free. It was not an easy decision, because the rents had realised about a hundred pounds a year towards the salary of a curate – a very necessary sum since St James' Church was unendowed.

Over the next few years every argument was used to further his aims. He arranged for special speakers from the Free and Open Church Association, and was particularly pleased in 1886 when a local M.P., Lord William Compton, became Vice President of the Association.

In 1883 he wrote:

I fear there is a falling off in the numbers of the congregation at the Parish Church and St Andrew's. I have no means of ascertaining exactly, but the number of coins contributed to the offertory acts as some guide, and the appearance of the Church from the pulpit or reading desk enables me to guess roughly the numbers present. I attribute the falling off at the Parish Church principally to the appropriation of Seats, which keeps the poor away; and I am strengthened in this belief by the fact that at St James' Church, where the seats are free, there is a decided increase.

He raised the question of safety, using the following example:

Another question of interest to those who worship in the Church is the means of exit in case of panic. The sad accident at Sunderland* has called attention to the dreadful consequences which may ensue if a crowd cannot find a ready egress from a building, and we cannot help fancying that the pew doors would be found almost as disastrous as the fatal bolt on the staircase there, in the event of a fire or a panic on a Sunday evening here. With a crowd rushing down the aisle it would be impossible to open the doors, which open outwards, and who knows how many 'pewholders' might be burned to death because they chose thus to fasten themselves in! Seriously, we recommend our readers to petition the Wardens to remove those inconvenient restrictions to freedom of entrance or exit.

Also, in 1883, he introduced a new idea.

SEATS IN THE PARISH CHURCH

A notice which is posted in the Parish Church, bearing date Easter, 1883, deserves a record in these pages. It runs thus – 'All the seats unoccupied when the voluntary is commenced are free, and may be taken by anyone.' This is signed by the four Churchwardens. It is noteworthy, first because it asserts the great principle that there are no such things as private rights in particular pews, and that all the seating of the congregation is in the hands of the Churchwardens. No pew can be attached to any particular house, or belong to any particular family, and appropriation by the Churchwardens may be made subject to any condition. In this case our Wardens have made the condition that if a person wishes to occupy the seat assigned to him, he must come in time for the commencement of the service; and much as we dislike Appropriation at all we think that this condition makes it less objectionable.

But it is noteworthy, secondly, because it puts an end to all 'turning out' at least after the organ has begun. No man has now a right to come after the commencement of Service, and say 'My pew, please, you must come out.' as we have heard of being done.

The Vicar has now arranged that the Organist shall play for nearly five minutes before the Choir and Clergy enter, with the object that those who have no seat may accommodate themselves then. We know one member of the Congregation who

---

* This refers to a dreadful tragedy, which took place in Sunderland in June 1883. Free toys were being given out on the stage of a local theatre. One hundred and eighty-three children scrambled down the staircase from the crowded gallery and were crushed against a locked door. A statue in memory of the disaster was restored in 2002.

waits in the porch until the first note is heard and then boldly takes an unoccupied place. We recommend many of our readers to do the same, and once seated on no account to move.

This offer had to be amended the next month by the following explanation:

It appears that some of our readers do not understand the word 'Voluntary' used in the notices in Church, to which we alluded in our last. The Voluntary is the piece of music played by the organist before the Service commences. The meaning of the notice, therefore, is that directly Mr Caseley begins to play all the Seats in our Parish Church are free.

The chance to fulfil his ambition came at last in 1886 when the galleries were dismantled, and the seating in the nave was rearranged. In his New Year's letter to the Parish in 1887, he paid tribute to the seat holders 'for their unselfish surrender of their seats', and declared all pews in Holy Trinity were unappropriated and free. He wrote, 'It is . . . the greatest blessing which has been granted to the Parish during my Ministry.'

Chapter 5

CHOIRS AND BELLS

Music in Church was important to George Arbuthnot. He thought it was an integral part of worship. As quickly as possible, he restored a daily choral evensong. Eventually he was able to reposition the choir stalls and the organ because he felt they were not heard to advantage in their old positions. He was well aware 'that the very best singers and most able musicians need constant and regular practice' and with this in mind he began to explore the idea of rewarding service in the choir with free education. He asked for boys of 'good social standing' to come forward, because he hoped to get rid of the strong local accent 'which sometimes marred the singing'. In the Autumn of 1881 he was able to open a Choir School. To begin with, the classroom at the Vicarage was used. Early in 1882 the following report was made:

The Choir School,
Stratford-on-Avon,
Warden, the Vicar of Stratford-on-Avon,
Headmaster, Mr J. A. Priest.

This school has now commenced its second term. It provides a sound Mercantile Education for boys destined for Commerce or Trade. It is conducted in temporary premises in Back Lane, where a large football and cricket field has been obtained. There is a Boarding House in connection with it, at the 'Choristers' House', Guild Street, where the Day Boys from the Country can dine if they like. The religious instruction is superintended by the Vicar, and an Examination is held annually by a qualified Examiner. Boys are received at any time. For Prospectus and full particulars apply to Mr J. A. Priest, Guild Street.

By December 1882 it was reported, 'This school, which has now been in existence a little more than a year, has so grown in numbers that it has been found necessary to engage the services of an Assistant Master. There are now forty boys, clearly showing that parents understand the benefits of a Commercial as distinguished from a Classical Education. Latin and French are taught as extras, but particular attention is directed to all that will be useful in a mercantile or business life.' That year they were examined in Religious Knowledge by the Rev. Charles Glynn, M.A. of Trinity College, Cambridge.

From then on, school reports were published regularly along with accounts of Open Days, Prize Days and Athletics Days. Sometimes the results of cricket and football matches were printed, too. In 1883 the Vicar wrote, 'The result of the

Christmas Examination has been very encouraging. The Headmaster (Mr Priest) is justly popular with both parents and boys. I do not wish this school to rival any older foundation in the town, but to supply the want which I think has been felt, of a school where Mathematics, and subjects necessary for a tradesman's life, are chiefly attended to, while the religious teaching is in strict conformity with sound Church principles.' And the following year he declared that the school was 'now taking a foremost place among the educational establishments of the neighbourhood'.

Candidates for the Choir School were accepted on the condition that they were given 'free education at the Choir School for one year – only paying for books and subscriptions to games fund. At the end of that time, if their voices and conduct are good they will be eligible for Choral Scholarships, which will provide them with free education until their voice breaks. Their parents will then be required to give an undertaking not to remove them from school until their voice breaks, and to allow them to sing whenever the Vicar requires them.'

Later the Vicar lowered the age of entry to eight, provided that the applicant could read well. Unfortunately, the arrangement did not last. The reasons for the 'friction' between the Vicar and the Headmaster are not given in the Parish Magazines, but in April 1890 the following announcement was made:

The Choristers' School

> A dual authority never works well. The Choristers' School, under the authority of the Vicar, and the Commercial Boarding School under the Headmaster, Mr Priest, have for some time been conducted together, meeting in the Vicar's Schoolroom in Back Lane and playing in his fields. This arrangement has given rise to disagreeable friction and therefore the Vicar has closed his schoolroom and arranged with the Rev. R. S. de C. Laffan to receive his Choristers at the Grammar School. There will be in future sixteen Choral Scholarships at the school; boys selected by the Vicar receiving an entirely free education in return for their singing at the Parish Church. Thirteen of these have been filled up and there are three vacancies, for which applications may be made to the Vicar.
>
> We understand Mr Priest will carry on the Commercial School at his own residence. Mr Priest is a good teacher and will no doubt be able to conduct the School satisfactorily, but as he and the Vicar could not work together, it was considered best that they should part before any mischief was done, and at Mr Priest's request, the Vicar has withdrawn his name from the list of patrons of the Commercial School and wishes it to be understood that he has no further connection with it.

Thereafter, the Grammar school received all the choristers who were awarded scholarships, although the arrangement was not without problems. In 1907 an announcement was given:

> Several requests have been made that boys in the Choir may leave before they are fifteen or their voice breaks. The Vicar has refused and held the parents to their agreement. It is not fair to the choirmaster that he should lose a boy's voice when it is at its best and he has spent so much pain upon its cultivation.

As well as free education, choristers could earn a little money every year. In 1896 the Vicar explained the sums involved:

> As some new boys are just about being admitted to the Parish Church Choir, this seems a suitable time to say something of the advantages of membership. What is it worth from a financial point of view, quite apart from the training which a Chorister receives? We will suppose a boy is nine years old when he is admitted, and that his voice lasts until he is fifteen. For the first three years he receives £2 a year, or £6 in all. When he is twelve he receives £3 a year, and when he is thirteen £5 a year, making in all for six years £19. Add to this his Concert money at Christmas, which may be said to average 10/-, and we have £22. Add to this his gratuity of 5/- a year if he leaves with a good character, and the total earnings come to £23 10*s*. There are not many boys who have earned more than £20 before they are fifteen, besides receiving a good education, and we are surprised that more parents do not see the advantage of getting a lad into the Parish Church Choir.

Another source of income was the annual Christmas Box. Before Arbuthnot's time it had been the custom of the Choirboys to go round Carol Singing, and for the money earned thereby to be divided between them. The Vicar was not fond of unregulated Carol Singing. 'He hoped that our Readers will not encourage the screeching which takes place in our streets during Advent under the pretence of Carol Singing. No Christmas Carols should be sung before Christmas Eve; and it is a good plan to give no money to children unless six come together. This centralizes and reduces the nuisance.'

The Vicar also thought that singing out of doors had a bad effect on boys' voices. The boys of St James' choir were allowed to continue to Carol Sing, but it was decided that an annual concert should be held by the Choirboys of the Parish Church each year. These were mostly very successful and after each performance a sum of money was given to each boy.

The report of the concert given in 1901 is typical.

CHORISTERS CONCERT

> The boys of the Parish Church gave their Christmas Concert rather later than usual this year. They had a bumper house, and collected over £18 which, after payment of expenses, the Vicar divided amongst them. We have no room for their programme, but mention that the items which seemed to give most satisfaction were a part song 'The Angel' by H. Coles, S. Lyons, W. Harris, and a solo 'My heart ever trusting' by E. Blackwell, together with Bogetti's Intermezzo by the band, which kindly gave their assistance. The following gentlemen of the Choir kindly helped the boys, Messrs R. Dixon, A. Andrews, D. Steel, W. Tompkins, J. Cranmer, D. Hill, A. Tompkins and H. Humphreys. The Rev. H. J. Gully also sang, and Mr Bloomer not only trained the boys but also accompanied the songs. After the concert the boys had supper with the Vicar and Mrs Arbuthnot.

There were a few less happy years. Once, ticket sales were so poor that the concert had to be cancelled. On another occasion, when the boys went round selling tickets they complained that doors were slammed in their faces and dogs were set on them!

At Christmas in 1891 eight boys staged a rebellion. The previous year there had been no concert because Mr Bloomer had succeeded Mr Casely as Organist. A subscription book was taken round and a larger sum than usual was raised. The Vicar kept back some of the money and staggered the payments, reasoning that the boys would like several smaller instalments spread over the year, rather than one larger sum.

Poor Mr Bloomer taught them some new songs all ready for the concert, when several of the older boys told him that if they didn't get all the money in one payment they 'would not sing their best'. This was too much for Mr Arbuthnot. The concert was abandoned, and the choristers were told that they must not go round Carol Singing. However, J. W. Brook, H. Large, H. Humphreys, J. Jelleyman, A. Ball, W. Rickatson, D. Steele and W. Barnacle disobeyed him. Of the remaining choirboys, some refused to go, because it had been forbidden, one was sick, and some were not asked to join in. The singers collected about £6 which was divided between themselves. When the Vicar demanded to see the subscription book, the ringleader. J. W. Brook, said it had been torn up! The last three boys saw the error of their ways and gave up their share of the money but the first five (backed by their parents) refused. The Vicar expelled them and appealed for contributions to give to the remainder of the choir. He pointed out that he organised treats, he entertained them frequently in his home, and he paid £40 each year in School Fees for them. He said:

> If the expulsion of a few boys now gains respect and obedience from the remainder we shall be better off for it, even though the singing may not be quite so strong as usual for a few months.

Certainly excursions were arranged, sometimes for the whole choir, at others men and boys had separate outings. Journeys were usually paid for by members of the Congregation, though one year only one donation was made towards the boys' outings. 'We fear the boys are not in good odour with the Congregation' was the comment.

The Vicar frequently provided the food, either supplying hampers of goodies or entertaining the members at a suitable restaurant. He also gave many suppers for the choir at the Vicarage – 'on teetotal principles'.

Men were needed, too. In 1883 the Vicar wrote, 'Both the Churches in the town are labouring under great disadvantages in the matter of music, by the difficulty we are experiencing in getting men to sing in their choirs. An instruction class for young men is about to be formed by the Rev. G. H. Moor, and I hope some who have voices, but as yet know little of music, will join it, and so qualify themselves for taking part in God's praises in Church. It seems sad that while the Choral Society is able to announce that it is increasing greatly in numbers, the Church Choir should be obliged to confess the opposite.'

Later he wrote, 'It seems hard that gentlemen are found always ready to sing at dinners, suppers, or penny readings while the service in Church suffers from such a want.'

For those who did join, the impression is given of a lively group who enjoyed their fellowship both in the music and the social life which grew out of rehearsals, festive services, diocesan festivals, excursions and suppers at the Vicarage.

This is an account of the excursion in 1898:

PARISH CHURCH CHOIR EXCURSION

The Annual Excursion of the Senior Members of the above Choir took place, as mentioned in our last issue, on Saturday, Aug. 28th. Hitherto, advantage has generally been taken of the excursions which in the summer run from Stratford. This year, however, the party made all their own arrangements and travelled by ordinary trains at the usual reduced pic-nic rates; and, although the expenses thus incurred were greater than those of the last few years, the generosity of subscribers was equal to the occasion. The place selected for the pic-nic was Haddon Hall, which is of easy access from Bakewell. . . . an excellent lunch was enjoyed, and, after inspecting the Hall, some drove on to Matlock Bath, where they were afterwards joined by the rest of the party who had returned to Bakewell, and all returned home in the best of spirits at 11.15 p.m., the 'aged men' of the Choir voting this year's excursion a record-breaker. The expenses amounted to £12 18*s*., the whole of which was subscribed.

He regarded the appearance of the choir as important, too. Every few years an appeal would be made to replace cassocks and surplices. Mrs Arbuthnot cut out several sets of surplices (the Vicar often paid for the material) and volunteers were asked to sew them up. In 1895 it was proposed that new cassocks, which were needed, should be 'purple like those worn by the Choristers of Lichfield Cathedral'. It was also decided that the organist should wear a surplice, too.

St James' Church had a choir, and a few recruits were enrolled at St Andrew's, Shottery, and All Saints at Luddington. These, too, were encouraged and appreciated, though they did not aspire to the excellence of the Parish Church. They also had their excursions and rewards. We hear of St James' Choir going on a very long trip to London. They left at 7.10 a.m. and returned at 5.00 a.m. the next morning. In the evening they had been to see the 'Original Christy Minstrels' in St James Hall, 'no doubt with the idea of picking up some wrinkles to improve the singing at St James''. At another time on the trip to Worcester, 'the party first attended Matins at the Cathedral. The Priest of St James' hoped his Choir would receive a musical lesson, but unfortunately his hope was very imperfectly realized. In the Anthem a considerable difference of opinion between Organist and Choir was manifested, which it is to be hoped will never take place at St James' Church. The opinion of the St James' Choristers seemed to be that they could "do better than that".'

After another outing, Shottery Choir was gently teased. On the homeward journey from Malvern, the party had proof 'that Shottery Choir CAN sing, if not always in tune'.

They were proud to announce 'Easter-day, 1883 will long be remembered at Shottery as the day on which the Choir first appeared in cassocks and surplices. These had been procured by the energy of the Rev. I. Daimpré, supported by the liberal offerings and industrious work of members of the Congregation.'

The choirs were much in demand for weddings and funerals, and members often provided musical items at concerts. Apart from the annual choirboys' Christmas Concert, St Cecilia's Day was observed as an Annual Festival, always followed by a social gathering at the Vicarage. The choir sometimes sang at Shakespeare's Birthday Celebrations as well.

Fund-raising concerts were given to buy psalters, hymn books and cassocks. In 1881 on Easter Day, the Vicar devoted the collection to a fund for the Improvement of Music.

When travelling in America, George Arbuthnot was interested in women's choirs which sang in Churches. He could not foresee that this would, in time, happen at Holy Trinity, but he did arrange for a group of Sunday School girls to sing at one additional service each month to save extra work for the choir. The boys were also given a 'holiday' for a month during the summer.

Some of the most exciting and rewarding occasions must have been the Diocesan Choral Festivals. This report appeared in 1883.

WORCESTER DIOCESAN CHORAL FESTIVAL

As most of our readers are aware, the Festival at Worcester, on June 7th, was a very great success.

A ready and generous response was made to the appeal for funds, and the choirs of the Parish were enabled to take part in the Festival. A short account of the day's doings, perhaps, may prove interesting. A start was made by the first train, to which, thanks to Mr Burchell's care, several extra coaches were attached. Worcester was reached by about 9.45 and, as all the choirs were expected to be in their places for the rehearsal by 10 o'clock, our Choirs proceeded at once to the Cathedral and no doubt the half-hour devoted to this did much good, and the Choirs got together.

There was some confusion before all the Choirs, numbering some 8,000 voices, were got into their places, but when this was accomplished all went well. As considerably more than half the singers took their places in the Cathedral before the Processional Hymn was sung, it went steadily and well. It was too evident that most of the Choirs were not accustomed to Processions, and slovenly, careless walking was the rule. Our readers will be glad to hear that the Stratford Choir compared most favourably with the others in their outward appearance and behaviour. It was most gratifying to see that the members did not forget the lessons of reverence which they had learnt at home, and evidently felt that they had come together to worship Almighty God, and not to take part in a huge concert. The Responses were arranged to be sung in unison by the great body of the singers, the harmonies from Tallis being sung by the Cathedral Choir. This had a very fine effect, though we doubted whether the harmony was quite strong enough. The Psalms were sung to single Anglicans, and went fairly well, one or two careless, badly-trained Choirs doing their best to spoil the chanting by hurrying. The Te Deum and Benedictus were taken to a Service composed for the occasion by the Rev. W. H. Woodward, Minor Canon of Worcester, and were very well sung. The morning Anthem was by Barnby, and was well adapted for such a service. Great effect was produced by introducing three short verses, sung by the Cathedral Choir. The Sermon was preached by the Rev. F. Holland, Canon of Canterbury, and was listened to with rapt attention. The Service was over by 1.30, by which hour all were ready for dinner. This had been ordered at Mountford's, and justice was done by all to the good things provided. After dinner, as there was quite an hour to spare before re-assembling for Evensong, some paid a visit to the China Works, some took a stroll through the City, while others took a well-deserved rest.

At 4.30 Evensong commenced, the music going even better than in the morning. The Canticles were sung to a setting by Lloyd, and the Anthem was 'From all that dwell below the skies', by Walmisley. The Hymns at both Services with the exception of the Processional (No. 319, Church Hymns), were not very striking, and went somewhat heavily. By six o'clock the Choirs were out of the Cathedral and, after a somewhat hasty cup of tea, the station was reached just in time to catch the 6.40 return train. To judge by the noise made by some of the more juvenile members of the Choir, the two long Services had not exhausted all vocal power though had the journey been much longer we think some fresh choristers would have been required at Stratford.

We must not omit to say that the Choir of St James' Church had a very handsome Banner presented to them, which they used on this occasion for the first time.

Many others followed at various venues. In 1884 the Parish Church played host to a smaller event when 200 choristers from the Coventry Diocese held a festival.

When one was held at Warwick in 1900, choir and congregation were recommended to cycle there.

Whatever pride George Arbuthnot took in the choir, he preached against 'professionalism', by which he meant going to Church as a duty, instead of for its own sake. He also warned the congregation that 'we go to Church, not as we should go to a concert to listen to music, but to worship Almighty God through it'. The congregation was urged to sing. When the choir was on holiday it was an 'opportunity for the congregation to sing out. More heartiness was needed, and all ought to use their voices to the best of their ability', he wrote. In 1903 he published a book containing the words of thirty anthems regularly sung by the Choir, priced at 6*d*. 'Worshippers will be glad to have one so as to be able to follow anthems intelligently.'

In January 1904 he paid the following tribute in his New Year Letter:

> I think that there are few, if any, Churches in the Diocese, after the Cathedral, where the music is better, and for this we are greatly indebted to the untiring devotion of the Organist and Choirmaster, Mr Bloomer. We must feel grateful, too, to the members of the Choir who give their services voluntarily for the glory of God.

CHURCH ORGANS

A great deal of effort was needed to acquire and maintain organs of a high quality in the Churches. All Saints, at Luddington, the newest of the Churches, was in the greatest need. The Rev. J. H. Beck enthusiastically worked to raise the money. It cost £100 and was built by Messrs. Hewins, a Stratford firm. It consisted of two manuals and pedal organ – twelve stops, and Parishioners were invited to see it at Hewins' workshop while it was being constructed.

It was opened on Wednesday, June 27th 1883 at 3.00 p.m. and the account records that 'its tones possess the sweetness for which Messrs Hewins' instruments are remarkable'. Although a steady downpour began before the service commenced, the Church was crowded. Many of the congregation had travelled considerable distances. The Choir of the Holy Trinity led the singing and their organist, Mr Caseley, played. Seven clergy attended. The Vicar preached taking as his text, Isaiah LX v.13: 'The glory of Lebanon shall come unto thee, the pine tree, and the box together, to beautify the place of my Sanctuary: and I will make the place of my feet glorious.' The hospitable Wilson family entertained everyone to tea in the barn, since the rain ruined any chance of tea on the lawn and games in the field. The time passed so pleasantly that many Stratford folk did not return home till midnight. The children got their treat the next day.

St James' Church needed a new organ, too. It was hoped that a good instrument would 'replace the worn-out "box of whistles" which at present hinders, rather than helps, singing at St James'. After much fund raising, Messrs Hewins were again asked to build the instrument. It cost £330 and was dedicated at the Harvest Festival Service in 1884. 'The instrument gave the greatest satisfaction, and it is confidently hoped that it will stand the test of time.'

The organ at Holy Trinity was situated in the North Transept, where it could not be heard properly. Many problems had to be overcome when it was repositioned but, in spite of all difficulties, the Vicar was determined to have an instrument of the highest quality to enhance the services of the Church.

THE BELLS

In the Vicar's opinion, the bell ringers of Holy Trinity had got into had habits. Characteristically he acted promptly and wrote down an account of the situation. This was only nine weeks after his induction.

February 1880

It is a good thing that this is a season when nobody wishes to be married, because necessary adjuncts of a festive wedding are now silent. Stratford is without any bellringers. The way this has come about is as follows: The old ringers have been in the habit of practising only during Advent, and then almost every night, much to the annoyance of persons who live near the Church. At other seasons they seldom touch the bells, except when they were paid to ring for some festivity. The Vicar, anxious to put an end to such a state of things, and having the legal control of the bells entirely in his hands, proposed to the men, that they should practise once a week for the greater part of the year, and should ring half an hour before one of the Sunday services. This should not entail the presence of all the ringers, but of a sufficient number to put the bells going. In return the Vicar promised to allow them to ring for any marriage performed in the Church, and for any other reasonable cause, and to demand whatever fee they liked for doing so. Also he agreed to head their subscription list at Christmas, and felt sure they would get much more under this plan than they had collected before. The ringers, however, did not see it in the same light and, believing that they would find the Sunday duty irksome, resigned in a body, and the Vicar accepted their resignation.

It is now desired to form a new body of ringers, and it is hoped that some Gentlemen of the town will volunteer their services. Mr Churchwarden Pearce has expressed his intention of joining, and will be glad of any who are willing to do so. We believe that the Reverend F. Smith contemplates learning the science of campanology, and we have always understood that, when once the rudiments are mastered, the pursuit of it is most engrossing.

Happily, for the remainder of his ministry, the ringers and the Vicar seemed to be on excellent terms. He regularly presided over their annual meetings in the belfry and appealed to the congregation to give generously to their annual 'Christmas Box'.

The Christmas Ringers go round with a book at Christmas to solicit support from inhabitants of the Parish and others. The Vicar wishes it to be known that this has his hearty approval and that he commends the appeal most strongly. The ringers ring our bells twice every Sunday for Public Worship, and receive no remuneration for their services, except the privilege of accepting a fee on certain occasions such as Marriages, and the election of the Mayor.

Two new bells were added in 1887 to commemorate Queen Victoria's Golden Jubilee. A set of handbells was given to the ringers by Mr John Hill.

There was some interruption to ringing during alterations to the Church, and in June 1903, steeplejacks, inspecting the spire, found that the tower and spire needed to be strengthened before ringing could be resumed.

The Reverend H. Collier published a poem on hearing the bells: 'Thoughts suggested by the Bells of Holy Trinity Church, Stratford-upon-Avon, ringing for early Service on the morning of Friday, August 12th, 1898.' Two of the verses read:

Ring out, sweet bells, for worship and for prayer,
Ring out o'er Avon's softly flowing tide;
Our hearts are heavy; soothe us in our care;
Tell us of joys that evermore abide.

Ring out sweet bells of Stratford, far and wide,
O'er mead and river, vale and upland ring;
Ring out for aye our anger, lust and pride,
And in their place love, hope and comfort bring.

Chapter 6

RENOVATIONS AND RESTORATIONS

In the first edition of the Parish Magazine, George Arbuthnot announced his intention of raising funds to renovate the Church. He wrote, 'Now, the first common object of interest which we possess is our fine old Parish Church, of which all inhabitants of Stratford are justly proud. But while we glory in its associations, I hardly think we can be proud of its present condition, and one of the most pressing needs of the Parish, which we must set before us, is its entire and thorough Restoration.' Throughout 1880, the Vicar tried to gain support for his aims of 'restoring the beauty of the internal arrangements and renewing the strength of its external walls'. Although the Bishop gave his warm approval, some Parishioners were not supportive, particularly those who did not agree to the abolition of pew rentals. Nevertheless, in October, he called a meeting at which a small committee was formed with the following members: Dr Kingsley, Mr E. Flower, Mr Nason, Mr North (Churchwarden), Rev. F. Smith and the Vicar. An eminent Church Architect, Mr Butterfield, was asked to make a report on the building and a public meeting was arranged to take place in the Town Hall on February 1st, 1881. The Bishop of Worcester was invited to attend.

Three resolutions were to be put to the meeting. 'That the present state of the Church is unworthy of its sacred purpose'; moved by the Marquis of Hertford; seconded by Mr Shirley of Ettington. 'The appointment of a Committee containing all the Members of the previous Committee and many more'; moved by Major Fortescue; seconded by the Hon. and Rev. Canon Leigh. 'Thanks to the Bishop'; moved by the rural Dean; seconded by Dr Kingsley. However, before any of these proposals could be made, a motion was proposed and carried, adjourning the meeting to that day three months. The names of the proposer and seconder are not given in the Parish Magazine.

The Vicar wrote with dignity that 'the conclusion at which the meeting arrived was a great disappointment to me and many others would be useless to conceal, and that if any indication of opposition had been given before, I should not have asked the Lord Bishop, the Marquis of Hertford, and others who came from a distance at considerable inconvenience to be present, is of course evident'. He listed and replied to the principal objections. Firstly, the Corporation had not been consulted. It was pointed out that the Mayor at that time, Mr C. E. Flower, had been asked to chair the meeting in October, and to serve on the Committee; both of these he had declined. The new Mayor was a Nonconformist and the Vicar had no idea that he would be interested in the proposed work, however, everybody would be able to join in the discussion and all plans would have to be approved at the Vestry Meeting. It was impossible to say that plans were being forced through. Secondly, it was said that the time was inopportune. The Bishop answered that the work was national and that assistance might even be sought from across the Atlantic. Thirdly, to the criticism that Stratford should be able to repair its own Church, it was said that this would depend on how much work was to be done.

A fourth objection was raised by Alderman E. Gibbs who thought that nothing was required to be done. He was alone in this opinion. The Vicar offered to make way for another man, but the Bishop desired him to continue in his efforts. It was decided to await Mr Butterfield's report and subsequently for the committee to be recalled. Then, the plans would be laid before the Parish assembled in the Vestry. 'While I intend to use every effort to restore the Church,' said the Vicar, 'I desire to act in accordance with the wishes of the Parish and in conjunction with the Corporation of the Borough.'

Gradually plans were made to begin the work. Extensive restoration was needed on the outside walls, and it was agreed that the galleries should be removed. The seating was to be re-arranged and a central aisle to be made. The High Altar needed remodelling, and the Choir Stalls and Organ were to be re-positioned. Other necessary jobs were: re-leading much of the roof, the re-glazing of the clerestory windows, and replacement of most of the flooring. An effort was to be made to fill the lower windows with stained glass. One ambitious project was to build a vestry on the site of the old Charnel-house. The churchyard also needed some attention.

Obviously, all of this could not be done at once, so the most pressing jobs were promoted first. By 1887 the tower had been strengthened and the peal of bells rehung. This included two new bells, added to commemorate Queen Victoria's Golden Jubilee. Much of the outside stonework had been repaired and the galleries removed. The total cost was £2,859 *0s. 0d.*

Meanwhile, work was being carried on in the chancel. The misericords were thoroughly cleaned and replaced, and new wooden panelling installed behind them. The High Altar was raised and enlarged, and an ancient altar slab of Purbeck marble (found buried in St Thomas's Chapel) became the mensa. Statues of St George and St Margaret of Antioch were placed in the empty niches on each side of the altar.

The next great effort was to repair the inside walls of the Nave, and to replace the pews on each side of the newly formed central aisle. At the same time, the floor was to be relaid, and the heating system improved. For several months in 1898, with the Bishop's permission, services were held in the Parish Parlour and the Town Hall, though some services were held in the Chancel. At last this major work was completed, though other jobs quickly followed. In 1903 a buttress had to be built to strengthen the north wall; in 1904 the Chancel roof had to be re-leaded, and in 1905 the Spire needed costly repair.

In 1879 there was little stained glass in the Church. In the Chancel about half the windows were coloured, including the East Window. The large windows in the transepts were plain, and the Nave had coloured glass in the Great West Window only, along with a few fragments of mediaeval glass in part of the Clopton Chapel.

The Vicar disliked the East Window, so he was particularly pleased when Mr William Law of Howesfield, Lancaster, undertook to replace it. The donor asked for some slight alterations to a proposed design: the figures of St Columba, St Aidan, St Patrick and St Cuthbert, were to be substituted for St Eric, St Columbus, Bp Seaburg and Wm Penn. These were readily agreed, and the finished window was unveiled by the Dean of Winchester in 1895. The old glass was adapted to fit the large North Transept window.

Matilda Morgan of Bromley, who had lived at 31 West Street, left £500 to pay for two windows. These were placed in the Chancel. One depicted 'The Beatitudes', and the other 'Eight Acts of Mercy' with illustrations taken from Old Testament sources. They were unveiled in 1889. Also in the Chancel was 'The Patriarchs' Window', given by Thomas and John Llewellyn Ryland in memory of their grandfather, John Ryland.

Ernest K. Baker gave the lower half of the window behind the Shakespeare Memorial, in memory of his uncle, J. O. Halliwell-Phillips, F.R.S., an eminent Shakespeare scholar. The subject was 'Elijah and the Prophets of Baal'. The money to glaze the large windows in the South Transept was given by Americans. The Vicar was very proud of this. The American Ambassador, Mr Bayard, came to Stratford on Shakespeare's birthday in 1896 to unveil it and give an address. The work was not complete at that date, since a further sum had to be raised, but everyone was pleased that such a prestigious gesture had been made. The debt was not finally cleared till 1905. Across in the North Transept in 1893, a much smaller window was filled with stained glass in memory of Emilie Minet. She had been the superintendent of the hospital and convalescent home. She was an indefatigable worker and much revered. The window depicts Elizabeth of Hungary.

Hoping that more stained glass would be given to beautify the Nave, in 1897, Arbuthnot propounded a plan

> to illustrate the history of the Church, subsequent to Bible times, by the characters we delineate on our windows. Thus the window of the Hodgson Family will show Christian Preachers, another represent Martyrs, another Virgins, another Confessors and so on, while the four-light window at the West will naturally contain figures of the four great Doctors, and the window in St Thomas' Chapel those of some of the Archbishops of Canterbury. Under each figure will be a scene from his life.

Much of this vision came true in the next eleven years. The Hodgson family began the scheme. They funded the 'Preachers' Window' in memory of two sons who died within two years of each other. Their example was followed by Mr Pritchard, who paid for the 'Physicians' Window' in the North Aisle. His father had been a well-known doctor in Stratford, and the gift was a memorial to his parents.

The Harding Family gave the 'Archbishops of Canterbury Window' in the Thomas à Becket Chapel in memory of Rev. Henry Harding, a former Vicar of Stratford. Sadly, Richard Fordham Flower lost his life in the Boer War. His family dedicated the 'Soldiers' Window' to him. The Hodgson Family used the figures of 'Faith, Hope and Charity' in the lower half of the Clopton Chapel Window in memory of Lady Hodgson, and filled the West Window in the South Aisle with 'an allegorical picture representing the reward of faithful service by a soldier of the Cross, whom St Michael is presenting to the Lord in Glory', in memory of Sir Arthur Hodgson. He and his wife died in 1902.

Another window was placed in the South Aisle in memory of Mr Bernard Newton Smith. He was the son of a former Curate at St James' Church and lost his life at sea. His window shows three founders of Monastic Orders.

The last window, which nearly completed the cycle of stained glass in the Nave, was in memory of Colonel James Neilson Potter of New York, U.S.A. He died in Stratford in 1906, and his family made this generous gesture.

Arbuthnot was delighted. In one of his many sermons following a dedication he said, 'And I remind you that even though the Preacher be dull, and the sermon uninteresting, you can learn a lesson through your eye, when you look at the lovely pictures with which your worship is surrounded.'

Two lights in the window in the North Aisle nearest to the porch were paid for by pennies collected by Sunday School children. They depict Saints Nicholas and Christopher. The third light and the next window were not coloured until Canon Melville's ministry.

In the porch is a small window dedicated to the memory of Arbuthnot's predecessor, Dr John Day Collis. His first wife is commemorated in another small window in the porch, but neither was buried in Stratford. All these personal bequests did much to beautify the Church.

New seats for the clergy and choir were paid for privately, too. In 1900, they were placed at the East end of the Nave, between the Clopton and Thomas à Becket Chapels. The Vicar's stall was the gift of Mrs Humphriss, in memory of her husband. She also gave the Litany Desk. The rest of the seating was very much an Arbuthnot Family affair. The sub-Vicar's Stall was given by the Dean of Lichfield (Mrs Arbuthnot's father). Mr C. G. Arbuthnot, the Vicar's cousin, gave the Precentor's Stall. The Vicar's mother, along with other members of their family, gave the stall next to the Vicar's, and Mr and Mrs Arbuthnot, aided by a few of their relations, gave the seats for the men and boys. They were dedicated on Lady Day, March 25th, by the Bishop of Zanzibar.

The gift of a pulpit did not go so smoothly. Helen Faucit was a much loved actress. By special invitation, for one performance only, she played Beatrice in 'Much Ado About Nothing' on the opening night of the theatre in 1879. In private life, she was the wife of Sir Theodore Martin, who, among other achievements, had written a biography of the Prince Consort. When Lady Martin died, he offered to pay for a new pulpit for the Church in her memory. It was a magnificent gift costing around £1,000 but the Vicar was disappointed with the materials and the design. He could never prevaricate and wrote in the magazine in 1900:

> I am sure the readers of the magazine will expect from me some tribute of gratitude to Sir Theodore Martin, for his handsome and pious (in the old sense) gift to our Church. I have never concealed my wish that it had taken the form of a handsomely carved pulpit, as being in my opinion, more in keeping with its surroundings, but as Sir Theodore and those who acted as his advisers thought

otherwise, I am free to confess that it would have been difficult to devise a handsomer marble one than that which now adorns the Church.

It was solemnly blessed and dedicated before a large congregation on St Luke' Day (October 18th) by the Bishop of Worcester, and the Master of the Temple Canon Ainger, preached the Sermon.

The organ proved to be an even greater problem. In February 1889 it wa moved from its position in the North Transept to the Eastern end of the Soutl Aisle. During the rebuilding, the huge case was placed over the arch at the Easter end of the Nave. While the work was being done the Vicar offered £5 towards a American Organ if five others of the Congregation would give a similar amount The cost was to be £100 and the Churchwardens felt that only part of the mone could be covered by the restoration fund. Alas, only two others were willing, so borrowed instrument was used for several months.

The opening of the new organ was postponed several times but finally 'the Ev of All Saints, commonly called 'Hallow E'en', was named for the ceremony and in spite of many difficulties, was adhered to', though the builders had not quit finished their work. Everyone was pleased with the sound produced by M Casely, the organist, and on the following Wednesday two recitals given by th Organist of Birmingham Town Hall created 'a favourable impression'. But th next Sunday, Mayor's Sunday, when a loyal Congregation rose to sing th National Anthem, the Organ positively refused to sound a note. It was reported 'Something had gone wrong with the engines; someone had blundered about screw; and our old friend, the American Organ, had to be wheeled out of it retirement once more to lead the singing.' The organ was never entirel satisfactory and in 1897 it was announced, 'Some correspondence has taken plac about this notorious instrument between the Vicar's solicitors and those of Messr Hill, the Builders of the instrument . . . As a result Messrs Hill have made proposal which they believe will cure the evils of which we all complain.' Th organ was therefore remodelled, and the bellows and engine removed from th Church to a building in the churchyard 'to get rid of that dreadful noise which i so disturbing to the congregation'.

A screen was erected across the East end of the South Aisle and, in 1906, Carved Oak Case was made for the part of the Organ that projected into the Soutl Transept. The following year an electric blower was installed.

Two other major gifts were made to the Church. The Rev. F. H. Hodgso erected 'a handsome Oak Screen across the North Aisle, marking off the old Lad Chapel which has been known for long as the Clopton Chapel'. The scree advanced a few feet beyond the original boundary of the Chapel, but Mr Hodgso signed a document which made it clear that no part of the floor of the Church wa alienated from the use of the Parish. The other gift was the beautiful Processiona Cross given in Memory of the actor, Frank Rodney.

There were many, many smaller presents over the years. Almost every mont some gift or other is recorded. At Christmas and Easter parishioners wer reminded of acceptable articles which could be given as presents to the Churche to mark the Festivals.

These were the requests made before Christmas in 1888:

CHRISTMAS PRESENTS

Who will give a Christmas Present to the Church?

At St James' the following are wanted: A new cover for the Credence Table. A handsome Dossal – the rod for it is already promised. An antependium for the Pulpit of Violet or Red. The Vicar can furnish particulars.

At the Parish Church – A Priest Surplice of fine linen, length about 30 inches. A cover for the Credence Table – the one in use is very shabby. Some new green alms bags. A small Patten and Chalice for use on Week Days. A dozen new Psalters for the Choir.

Flowers will be needed at all the Churches for Christmas Decorations. Holly will also be very acceptable.

The following list gives thanks for the Easter gifts to St James'.

An unusual number of gifts were given to the Church. The donors do not wish their names to appear, but it is right to say that one lady was an especial benefactor.

The gifts comprised: White and gold hangings for the Altar, beautiful lace for the super-frontal, carpet for the floor and kneelers for the priests' stalls, white markers for the lectern, curtains for the organ chamber, a beautifully worked fair linen cloth for the Altar, and psalters and hymn-books for the Choir-men, and hymn-book for the organ desk.

Two ladies gave Mr Wilson a beautifully smocked surplice.

The Churchwardens re-carpeted the pulpit stairs.

During Lent the Congregation provided new violet hangings for the Altar. A lady of the congregation made both sets of hangings and the curtain, and, although she received assistance, the bulk of the work fell upon her.

Altogether Easter 1906 is a Festival much to be remembered at St James'.

These are typical of many appeals, and appreciation of all that was given.

There was so much to be done on the Parish Church it would have been a blessing if the other three Churches under Arbuthnot's care had been in good order, but unfortunately each of these had problems.

St James' Church had only been consecrated in 1855 but the construction had been poor, and in 1879 the spire and vestry had not been built. Cracks appeared in the walls and, after an inspection in 1883, the following report was made:

> We are informed that the condition of the building of this Church turns out to be worse than was anticipated. It is hardly creditable that in some places the foundations are only two feet below ground, and no drain to carry off the surface water. The consequence is the foundations have sunk and must be underpinned. The sum named for this is approximately £500, which is, we fear, far beyond the resources of the congregation. Consequently an appeal must be made to the general public and, considering the importance of the work, it should not be made in vain.

With great effort the money was raised and the work carried out, and the Chancel was extended also.

Further expense was necessary when dry rot was found in the South Transept, and a new organ had to be provided.

Once again, some furnishings were provided by private donors. Lady Emil Harding gave a window in memory of her husband, who was the Vicar o Stratford at the time when the Church was built.

St Andrew's Church, Shottery, was consecrated in 1870 and the structur appears to have been reasonably sound, but some decorative features were added These included several stained glass windows and, at different times, a Chance Screen (in 1889) and a Pulpit (in 1896). The Screen was designed by Miss France but the woodcarving of the Screen and Pulpit were executed by Mr Horsman o Shipston Road.

A particularly generous gift was a new Curate's House which was built in 190 at the expense of Mr T. Miles of Mount Pleasant. He and his wife had alread given two of the stained glass windows. The congregation worked to raise th money to enlarge the Vestry.

All Saints' Church at Luddington was the newest of the Churches. In his repor for 1882, the Vicar declared it to be 'a most complete little village Church, barrin the want of a Choir and congregation'. It also needed an Organ, which wa installed in 1883.

At Holy Trinity, the churchyard needed constant attention. It was closed fo burials in 1882. Within a year the Corporation were claiming the freehold, bu eventually it was agreed in favour of the Vicar. He used the following case fron the local court to back up his side of the argument:

The Churchyard

> The Mayor gave an important decision last month affecting the ownership of the Churchyard. A man was brought before him who was found lying dead drunk by the path from the North gate to the Waterside, the charge being that of drunkenness in a public place. The man pleaded guilty, but the Mayor dismissed the case on the ground that this foot-path is not a public place. We do not question the correctness of the Worship's decision, but it clearly shows the Vicar can close the walk by the Terrace when he chooses. The only public path through the Churchyard is a four foot way from North to South passing the West End of the Church. Of course it does not follow that the other paths will be closed, as to do so would be a most unpopular and impolitic move, but never-the-less the right exists.

In 1887 the New Jubilee Avenue to the West Door of the Church was opene to commemorate Queen Victoria's Golden Jubilee, and in 1889 new Churchyar Gates were erected at the cost of nearly £100. This was largely met by the Visitors Fund, but Mr Edward Flower, whose carriage accidentally destroyed the old gates kindly gave £10. They were made by Messrs Jones & Willis of Euston Road London, of wrought iron and rich workmanship. In 1906 when Colonel Potter o New York, U.S.A. died in Stratford, Mrs Potter fitted up part of the building o the south side of the churchyard as a Mortuary Chapel, until the corpse could b moved to the family vault at Pau in France. She generously presented the hanging of violet and white to the Church, and it became the last resting place of man parishioners until their day of burial. This was of immense benefit to familie living in small houses.

The completion of almost every one of these improvements was accompanie by a service of dedication. These varied from a few prayers during a normal service to a 'special' service with choir, organ and visiting preacher.

Wherever possible, first class craftsmen were used. Several windows were made by Heaton, Butler & Bayne, and two were designed by Kempe. The organ was built by Messrs Hill. It is obvious that this work was divided between various craftsmen. After one delay it is noted 'as usual where several persons are employed, the blame is cast from one to another until it is difficult to say who is really at fault'. The architects were Bodley & Garner, and G. F. Bodley was responsible for much of the design. The magazine reported the great honour he was awarded in 1889:

> Those who take an interest in our Church Restoration, will be pleased to read of the honour conferred on our Architect, Mr Bodley. About £1,200 is still required to pay for the work already done at the Church, and some more to complete Mr Bodley's designs.
>
> A meeting of the Royal Institute of British Architects was held in the Institute Rooms, Conduit Street, on June 27th, for the presentation to Mr G. F. Bodley, A.R.A., of the Royal Gold Medal for Architecture. The medal was first presented by Her Majesty at the instance of the Prince Consort, in 1848, for the encouragement of architecture, and in each succeeding year it has been conferred upon some distinguished architect or man of science or letters. In the absence through illness of Professor Aitchison, the chair was taken and the presentation made by Mr W. T. Fawcett, who spoke of Mr Bodley as a true artist.

It will be noticed that even in the middle of the congratulations an appeal for funds is made. Unfortunately, Mr Bodley agreed to use marble for the new pulpit instead of wood; indeed, he designed it, and the Vicar was very disappointed. Bodley died in 1907, and the design of the pulpit was still an annoyance.

> The death of Mr G. F. Bodley, R.A., the architect under whose case our Church was restored and beautified during the last 20 years cannot be allowed to pass unnoticed. We regret that he allowed himself to permit the pulpit to be introduced, which although stately in itself, is in our opinion, unsuited to its surroundings, but regarded as a whole his work for us was of a nature which accorded with his position as the foremost architect of the day, and we sincerely mourn his decease.

All these alterations cost money. In some cases families and friends paid for a particular piece of work like a window or a seat, but mostly cash had to be raised. The Visitors' Fund, made up of donations given by tourists entering the Chancel to view Shakespeare's grave, accounted for some of this. Lots of special efforts were arranged, such as concerts, bazaars and recitals, and the proceeds were added to the fund. One prestigious event which raised £45, was a recital of Dickens' *A Christmas Carol* by Sir Squire Bancroft. Sir Arthur Hodgson promoted a 'charming concert which was given at The Memorial Theatre on the Queen's Birthday'. It was given by the Ladies Haresfoot Orchestra, and the fund benefited by another £100.

By far the largest amount was given in private donations, some of them from overseas. Locally, the Hodgsons, Philips, Hardings and Nasons led the way with generous subscriptions. C. E. Flower offered £1,000 conditionally, anc Edgar Flower added another £200. The Corporation gave £210. The Vicar gav £10 on this occasion, but he gave up his claim to over £100 a year from the Churcl Visitors' Fund. A Ladies Committee was formed, and their fund-raising paid fo a good deal of work in the Chancel. H.R.H. the Prince of Wales sent 20 guinea with a 'kind and gracious letter'.

By 1890 £4,783 had been spent. Nine years later further funding was neede for more extensive work. A large sum was borrowed. Archibald Flower stoo security for a third of the sum, Arbuthnot for another third, and Arbuthnot witl Mr Nason and Sir Arthur Hodgson for the rest. When the work was finished, a amount was still outstanding to be paid, and in 1903 Miss Marie Corelli* generously gave the remainder.

One important piece of rebuilding was never achieved because of the lack o funds. A new Vestry had been planned on the site of the old Charnel-house. Thi must have been a great disappointment to the Vicar.

Arbuthnot's efforts to restore and arrange Holy Trinity were, on the whole well received by his congregation; but he did get some adverse criticism from eve as far away as America. In a publication called *Shakespeareana* it was said, 'In 188 came a tremendous "restoration" so drastic as to rouse the entire world to protes and to ridicule.' The same writer quoted Mr William Winter who had sent a lette to the *New York Tribune* saying that 'Vicar Arbuthnot was making the inside o Shakespeare's Church look like a beer-garden'.

Fortunately, the Vicar also received much support. This letter was quoted i the magazine in 1899:

> My dear Sir,
>
> Visiting your Church twice last month, I was delighted with the changes made, since I saw it last, nearly twenty years ago. I venture to send a contribution towards the work still to be done. I think it is difficult to exaggerate the good that may be done to the thousands who visit Stratford, by the picture you have given them of a sanctuary of the Church of England, in its true and best aspect. Believe me to be,
> Yours faithfully

The writer was a Fellow of an Oxford College. He did not wish his name to b given in the magazine.

---

* Marie Corelli was a highly successful writer of popular novels. She lived in Stratford.

Chapter 7

THE SHAKESPEARE CONNECTION

George Arbuthnot realised that the presence of Shakespeare's grave in Holy Trinity Church was a mixed blessing. He quickly made his opinions known.

> We have a great name to trade upon in our National Poet, who lies buried here, but we must not forget that the building is the Church of Almighty God, and not a mere monument erected to the fame of a man, however illustrious.

Certainly, thousands of tourists came. In 1889 twenty-eight thousand, five hundred and sixty-four visited the grave – only four hundred less than the number who went to the Birthplace. Many did not understand how a church conducted worship. One Good Friday it was reported that a visitor had said it was impossible to see the Church since a service was going on all day! In the face of this kind of misunderstanding the Vicar wrote:

> It always appears to me that Stratford Church stands in quite a different position to all other Parish Churches in the land. Of course in this statement I do not include Cathedrals or College Chapels. It is visited by thousands, who rarely if ever enter a Church of worship; by hundreds from America and other countries, who know little or nothing about an English Parish Church; by many, who are outside our communion, and do not understand our Service; to all these it is a specimen of what an English Parish Church professes to be. Surely, then, we, to whom the care of it has been entrusted, should be anxious to keep it in such a state as to impress every Visitor with the dignity of Anglican Worship, and to put before the most careless, 'the beauty of holiness' . . . Stratford Church must be made a typical Church, and must be maintained as such, and all the Services in it must be dignified and impressive.

Although he would have wished entrance to the Church to be free, after consideration he decided to make a charge:

> Our Church is visited daily, at least in summer, by great numbers of strangers, who come not to pray, but to see the grave of our great Poet. Were they worshippers, there can be no doubt that it would be monstrous to subject them to any charge, but they come solely as sightseers, and I really do not see why people should not pay to see Shakespeare's grave, as much as to see his house. At all events, my predecessor instituted a charge of sixpence for every visitor to the Church, and this is now a considerable augmentation to the income of what is really a poor living. Even if I could afford it, which I cannot, I think I should be wrong to prejudice the rights of

> my successor, by giving up a perfectly legitimate source of income. But I hope the plan is capable of some modification, and I desire to give all who wish to visit the Church solely for the sake of prayer an opportunity of doing so without any difficulty. I propose therefore that the Nave should be left open to all comers free of charge, from Matins until Evensong, except during the Attendant's dinner hour, and that a charge for admission should be made on all except parishioners, who enter the Chancel or Vestry. This will enable all who wish merely to see the Church generally, to do so without payment, but those who come to visit the Poet's grave, or to inspect his entry in the Register, will have to pay for the privilege of doing so. The charge will be a fixed one for every person, and for this year, after the payment for the Attendant's salary and other necessary charges, I will devote the balance of the money thus obtained as my subscription to the Fund for the Restoration of the Church.

It was during Arbuthnot's incumbency that the regular annual birthda celebrations developed. At the end of April each year there was a season of play at the Memorial Theatre. It became the custom of the Mayor and othe dignitaries, with the pupils of King Edward's School, to take flowers and wreath to the Church on Shakespeare's birthday, April 23rd*. Visitors who had come t the town to see the plays joined in. The procession went into the nave where short sermon was preached before the flowers were taken up to the sanctuary t the accompaniment of the organ. By 1907 this event had become so popular tha entrance to the nave was by ticket only.

Each year on the Sunday nearest to the birthday, the Vicar invited distinguished preacher to deliver the 'Shakespeare Sermon'. Among those wh came were: the Bishops of Ely, Bristol, Ripon, Worcester, and Derry. The Bisho of New York accepted an invitation in 1897, but was unfortunately unable to kee the appointment, though he came later on in the year. Canon Luckock preached He later became Dean of Lichfield (and George Arbuthnot's Father-in-law).

Others were Canon Ainger, the Master of the Temple, and Canon Skrine 'himself a poet, who has won the Newdigate Prize at Oxford'. Possibly, the mos prestigious was the Very Reverend the Dean of Canterbury, Dr Farrar, who cam in 1900. His address, along with seven others, was published in a book o 'Shakespeare's sermons' in 1900.

Two of the Vicar's own sermons, preached at Evensong on birthday Sunday were included. In the *Church Times* a reviewer wrote, 'Dr Arbuthnot had no nee to apologise for the introduction of two of his own sermons into the collection for each proves his fitness for his vocation as pastor of the congregation of whic Shakespeare was a member, and as a Vicar of the church which contains his tomb.

In 1889 a 'Shakespeare Stamp', on which was a picture of 'the bust', was sold Each cost a shilling, and any letter weighing less than half an ounce could b posted in the church porch, and sent to any address in the world. Presumably official stamps were affixed as well.

---

* The custom of laying flowers on Shakespeare's grave seems to have begun in 1769 at the 'Jubilee Celebration led by David Garrick..

Two gifts with theatrical connections were made to Holy Trinity at this time. Helen Faucit* had been a very popular actress. Although she had retired, she agreed to play Beatrice in 'Much Ado About Nothing' on the first night of the opening of the Memorial Theatre in 1879. When she died in 1898, her husband, Sir Theodore Martin, offered to give a new pulpit to the Church in her memory.

The Processional Cross was given in memory of Frank Rodney.† He was an actor with Frank Benson's Company, which came regularly to the Memorial Theatre, and was extremely popular with Stratford audiences. He gave his last performance there as Buckingham in Henry VIII in 1902. He knew that he was suffering from an incurable condition, and his final lines were terribly poignant:

> All good people,
> Pray for me! I must now forsake ye
> Farewell.

His family and friends, and members of Benson's company subscribed to give the Cross as his memorial. On it is inscribed another line from the play.

> Make of your prayers one sweet sacrifice,
> And lift my soul to heaven.

George Arbuthnot was extremely proud of Holy Trinity's connections with Shakespeare. At the beginning of his ministry, when alterations were to be made to the interior of the Church, a rumour was started that he intended to 'interfere' with the poet's grave. He was very indignant at such a suggestion.

He personally acted as guide to many distinguished visitors including, in 1895, The Prince of Wales (later King Edward VII).

He was interested in the life of the Bard. At the opening of the Parish Parlour, which he built for the use of the Church to celebrate Queen Victoria's Diamond Jubilee, he gave a talk on 'The Life of Shakespeare', illustrated with 'Limelight Views'. He certainly attended the theatre, on one occasion taking the Dean of Canterbury, Dr Farrar, and his wife. Ben Greet's Company of Pastoral Players performed on the Vicarage Lawn and, in 1895, 'As You Like It' was played there. However, in 1908, he objected strongly to a production of 'Measure for Measure' being mounted at the theatre. He considered it quite unsuitable for a lady to see. He had evidently written a letter to the *Herald* expressing his opinion and he repeated this in the magazine:

> I have challenged them (the readers) to say that any of them will take a young lady to see it, and all I can do now is to state my opinion that no respectable and modest woman ought to go to it. I am sorry if this statement advertises it, but as Vicar of this Parish I feel obliged to make it.

As a trustee of the Birthplace, Arbuthnot worked to get concessions for the townsfolk. In 1883 this item was printed:

---

* The Memorial to Helen Faucit, which Sir Theodore wished to place in the Church, is in the Art Gallery in the Swan Theatre.

† Frank Rodney's portrait as Buckingham can be seen in a stained glass window at the Swan Theatre.

We are glad to see that the Trustees of New Place have at last partially carried out the resolution which was passed on the Vicar's suggestion, at their annual meeting last year, by opening the Gardens on Monday, Wednesday, and Saturday, free of charge. All our readers, especially the young ones, should know this, and avail themselves of the boon conferred upon them by the kindness of the Trustees.

In 1887 it was reported:

By kind permission of the Trustees the Vicar has during the past month conducted parties of the elder children at the National School, forty in all, over the Birthplace and Museum. The children were much interested, and afterwards retailed their impressions in very nice letters to Mrs Arbuthnot. Not one of them had been in Shakespeare's House before, and it seems an extraordinary and lamentable thing that more than half the population – we think we may say nine-tenths of Shakespeare's native town – have never entered his house, or seen the Museum of his relics. Surely something might be done to dispel the ignorance or lethargy which causes this.

He wrote and published a series of short guides to the town. He had n 'pecuniary interest', his object was to show visitors how to spend a few hour pleasantly in his Parish.

He seems to have wished to be an ambassador for Stratford on some occasion when he travelled abroad, and he wrote many letters to his parishioners. He too a keen interest in anything connected with Shakespeare. From Venice he wrote 'Almost next to our hotel on the Grand Canal is the house of Desdemona' and h added at the end of his letter:

I must add a postscript at Verona to say we have visited and dropt a tear at the tomb of Juliet, and seen her house with a very unclimbable and inaccessible balcony, and also the home of Romeo. All traces of the Two Gentlemen seem to be lost.

In Florence he watched flowers being laid on a stone on the pavement. H discovered that it was the spot where Savonarola was martyred. 'The scen brought back what had happened in our own dear town exactly one month before and we were glad to be there, for the great Florentine is worthy to b commemorated as we do our William.'

While on holiday in Scotland in 1897, Arbuthnot visited the home of Rober Burns in Ayr. He wrote, 'Burns is the great Poet of the Scottish people and stand to them as Shakespeare does to us. He has not influenced the world a Shakespeare did, nor stamped his mark on the language of the English speakin race. In one respect he did resemble Shakespeare. He was essentially a man of th people.'

In preparation for his visit the Vicar obtained, through Mr Richard Savage, Wreath of laurel and flowers picked from the garden at the Birthplace. This h hung in the room where Burns was born. He was shocked to find that the numbe of visitors in Ayr exceeded the number visiting Henley Street – though th comparison seemed to please the custodian. The following Sunday he preached i Holy Trinity Church in Ayr. On his tour of America in1894, he lectured severa times to raise money for the American window in Holy Trinity. He preached onl three times, though he did not lack invitations. One sermon was given at Port Huron where he took the service for the Rev. John Munday, who had preached in Stratford two years before. In Boston he passed the University – 'endowed by John Harvard, whose grandfather, Alderman Rogers, lived in Stratford'. He also visited the home of Longfellow, where he was delighted to find, in the room where the poet worked, 'the bust of the immortal William'.

Chapter 8

THE SCHOOLS

In 1880, the main schools in Stratford were: the Boys' Grammar School (Kin Edward's), the National Schools on the Alcester Road and at Shottery (Church o England), the British School (Nonconformist), the Roman Catholic School, an Mrs Flower's Infant School. The latter closed almost immediately because it wa not up to standard. There were about 750 places at the National Schools and 10 at the Roman Catholic.

Shortly after Mr Arbuthnot's arrival it was announced that a Publi (Undenominational) Elementary School was to be established. The Vicar wa very much opposed to this, firstly because he believed that all children shoul have schooling where Religious Education was based on the Bible, the Creed an the Catechism, and secondly, because Anglicans and Catholics already supporte their schools financially, he saw no reason why they should pay extra rates to fun another school. 'The school, if created,' he said, 'will bring ill-will and extr expense.' His immediate, practical response was to enlarge the premises of th National Schools to make an extra 175 places.

Children attended school between the ages of five to thirteen, but it wa possible to leave earlier if all tests up to the fifth standard had been passed. A fe of three pence a week was charged for infants in Standards 1 and 2. For the Uppe Classes, Standards 3, 4, 5 and 6, the sum was four pence for each pupil. If three o more children in a family attended, a reduction of one penny for each child wa made. The charges were also to be made by the new Board School, so no benef was to be gained by changing schools.

By the end of the century, education was free.

Once it was seen that a Board School was to become a reality, the Vicar wa determined that out of seven possible places for local people on the Boar appointed to run the school, the Anglicans should fill four of them. His theor was that the Church Schools educated more than twice the number of pupils i other schools, and that therefore there were over twice as many rate-payers wh were Anglicans, so the proportion of Church of England Members on the Boar would be correct. A compromise was reached. He got his wish; he and Messr Deer, Hodgson and Kingsley were from the Church; Messrs Eaves and Winte were from the Nonconformists, and the Rev. J. Shutter came from the Roma Catholics. However, the Vicar was disappointed that he was not elected to th Chair, and the Roman Catholic Clergyman became Vice-chairman. There was further setback when Mr F. Thompson was elected as Clerk in preference to th man nominated by the Vicar. One of their first duties was to agree on the kind o

Religious Teaching to be followed in the New School.

The School began in the old British School in Rother Street, but the building was in poor condition, and other premises had to be found. A new building was erected in Chestnut Walk, and the British School staff were re-engaged. The sum of £242 had to be found. 'Thus the rate-payers are beginning to experience the delights of having a rate-supported school,' wrote Arbuthnot.

Every third year the board had to be re-elected. Arbuthnot made it known that he did not wish to stand unless three fellow Anglicans were appointed too. In the election, the Vicar and *four* colleagues were successful, and this time, Arbuthnot was elected Chairman, and Mr Deer became Vice-chairman. After a further three years, one Anglican was dropped in favour of a Nonconformist, otherwise, for fifteen years the constitution of the Board remained, with the Vicar in the Chair.

In 1896, the Board, under Arbuthnot's leadership, had refused to appoint a Unitarian teacher. Rumours were spread that she had been dismissed because of her beliefs, but as the Vicar said, this was untrue, because she had never been appointed. In consequence, in 1899, when the Board was due for re-election, Mr Talbot, a Unitarian, offered himself for election and, to the Vicar's 'great disappointment', he not only took a seat, gaining twenty more votes than Arbuthnot, but pushed one of the Church candidates off the Board.

Three years later the 'Church Party' debated whether or not to try to restore four members to the Board. The Bishop Suffragan gave his opinion that the existing state need not be disturbed as long as the Church held the Chairmanship. The situation altered in 1903 when all the schools in the Parish were taken over by the Education Authority of the County Council. The Board School was now to be called a 'Provided' School and the Vicar was appointed to the Board of Managers again. He viewed the changes with mixed feelings. Because the Church Schools would now receive some money from the rates, his Parish would not have to raise so much, but some independence would be taken out of his hands. Evidently some 'dissenting friends' were grieved that Church Schools would be rate-supported. The Vicar urged them to remember the previous twenty years 'when we' (the Church people) had 'cheerfully paid a rate of sixpence in the pound to support the Board School where their children have found education which has satisfied them'. He continued to fight for the kind of education he believed in. In 1907 he was fighting a proposal that the Church and R.C. Schools should pay a proportion of their teachers' salaries calculated on the time devoted to denominational religious teaching. By then he did not teach so often in the schools personally, but certainly supervised the work of his curates as they took their share of taking classes.

Inspections

The Schools at Alcester Road and Shottery were each inspected twice a year, once by Her Majesty's Inspectors of Schools, and once, because they were Church Schools, by the Bishop's Inspector. The results of these were always printed in the Magazine.

The following article, printed in 1894 is typical of an H.M.I.'s report for Alcester Road:

THE SCHOOLS

The Managers of the National Schools have received the following Report on the state of the School from H.M. Inspector. It is a gratifying Report, both for the Managers and the Teachers, and should be read with great satisfaction by the parents of children attending the School.

Boys' School. – The discipline is good, though that of the third Standard seems to have suffered from the loss of its teacher. The teaching of the boys to read to themselves is worthy of special praise. The Dictation, Composition, and Recitation have been well and carefully taught. The Arithmetic is fairly good, that of the fifth Standard being only fair. The class subjects of the First and Fourth Standards are not as generally known as elsewhere. The Note-Singing is good, but the songs do not reach last year's level.

Girls' School. – The tone of this School is very pleasant. Taking into consideration the not very liberal provision of staff, the Headmistress may be congratulated on the work done, and it would be wrong to blame her because the higher principal Grant cannot be recommended. The girls read with expression, though they might well display a greater understanding of the subject matter. The writing has fallen off to some extent, especially in the Fourth Standard. Spelling is fair. Composition is pretty good. The Arithmetic is fairly good. Recitation has been well taught. The Geography of the Second Standard deserves special praise. The Needlework is maintained at a high standard.

Infants' School. – Discipline and Singing by note, good. Elementary Subjects and Object Lessons, good. Needlework, Knitting, and other occupations, good; and general efficiency, very good.

The Bishop's Inspector naturally concentrated on the religious side of the school curriculum. This report is from Alcester Road in 1889.

THE NATIONAL SCHOOLS

The following gratifying Reports have been received by the Vicar from the Bishop's Inspector. We ought all to feel much obliged to the Rev. Hunt for the pains he takes not only in examining the classes but in arranging the children in order of merit. In the upper divisions, all who are in the first class will receive prizes from the Managers, on condition that they compete for the Diocesan prizes in Lent, and all who are mentioned in the lower standards will have certificates.

Boys' School. – Number on register, 292; presented for examination, 278. Division I (71): Catechism and Bible, excellent. Division II (95): Catechism, Bible and Christian Year, excellent. Division III (112): Catechism, Bible and Prayer Book, excellent. Summary: I am glad to be able to report each division and each subject excellent. The work of the two lower divisions is quite unexceptionable. In the upper division I think I have known a higher standard reached, but there was scarcely a failure, and the number of boys in this part of the School is as exceptionable as it is satisfactory. A little more accuracy in New Testament knowledge is to be desired, e.g. the Presentation of our Lord was very generally confused with the Circumcision. Discipline and tone are admirable. The School ranks high in Class A.

Girls' School. – Number on register, 250; number presented, 236. Division I (62): Catechism and Bible, excellent. Division II (89): Catechism, very good; Bible and Christian Year, excellent. Division III (85): Catechism, Bible and Prayer Book, excellent. Summary: Some of the writing out of Catechism in Standard II was not as accurate as it might have been. That is the only criticism I have to make on the work of this School. The Bible knowledge throughout is quite excellent: and the girls generally have been thoroughly well grounded in Church doctrine. The enclosed class list shows that of 85 girls examined in Division III, 48 obtained a mark of merit, while only 5 failed. The number placed in class I in Standard IV is specially creditable. The School stands very high in Class A. Discipline and tone are excellent.

Infant School. – Number on register, 280; number presented, 215. Division I (130): Excellent. Division II (85): Excellent. Summary: All the work in this School deserves the highest praise. The answering in the upper division is exceptionally bright and intelligent; throughout the repetition is quite accurate and distinct. The children obviously enjoy their school life. I do not know a better infant department.

The Infant department at Alcester Road rarely had a poor report. The H.M.I.'s wrote in 1889, 'The Infants are as good as ever. The School is conducted with brightness, energy and skill, and instruction is thorough.'

Shottery School was much smaller and seems to have suffered from frequent staff changes. In 1903 the situation was particularly bad.

Mixed School. – the way in which the School is staffed renders effective organisation almost impossible, and it is surprising that even tolerable progress has been made.

Infant Class. – Some pretty good work has been done here, but object teaching seems to be of little value, and the arrangement by which the teacher in charge of the class leaves it for two half-days a week is unsatisfactory.

The reports also touch on the state of the buildings and the need for further extensions. An enormous effort was made in 1881 to provide extra classroom space at Alcester Road School. At Shottery the previous year an H.M.I. wrote, 'I earnestly draw the attention of the Managers to the desirability in the interests of the School of enlarging the present Infant Classroom. The Classroom is too small, and justice will not be done to the little children until it is enlarged.' At Alcester Road in 1900 we are told, 'The small, dark classroom cannot be recognised as part of the accommodation.' For some reason it was suggested that a museum should be provided in the girls' department.

Cloakroom space was often deemed inadequate, that at Alcester Road had to be doubled in size.

Playgrounds always needed attention: the boys' at Alcester Road was a swamp in wet weather, and the girls' at Shottery was muddy. The lavatories ('Offices') were a constant source of complaint. At Alcester Road 'offices were wrongly situated immediately below the window'. At Shottery the boys' lavatory was not drained 'and should be remedied without delay'. Again at Shottery it was reported that the boys' offices were not in a sanitary condition, and of those for the infants at Alcester Road we are told, 'the seats in the offices are not separated'.

One nice comment is made of Alcester Road; when new cloakrooms were provided, the lavatory was moved to what had been 'the coal-hole' – 'a curious transformation'.

Not only the pupils were inspected. Both Schools trained pupil teachers. Sometimes as many as ten young people were employed. At Alcester Road in 1898 the boys had a Headmaster, four assistants and two pupil teachers, the girls a Headmistress, three assistants and four pupil teachers; and the infants had a Headmistress, three assistants and three pupil teachers.

Sometimes vacancies for pupil teachers were advertised. Fourteen year-olds who had passed all their grades, and who were respectable and well-behaved, could apply. The starting salary for boys was £10 a year rising annually by £2 10*s*. When qualified, by the age of 23 a young man could be earning £50 to £80 each year depending on whether or not he had been trained at college. The Vicar urged scholars and parents to consider such a career. Teaching was an honourable profession and a responsible job.

The reports on the pupil-teachers and their examinations were also printed. They were always expected to do well, and mostly they achieved a high standard. Mediocre marks were rewarded with comments like 'the results were not quite good enough for Stratford'. However, usually there was praise all round. In 1885 the magazine was proud to print, 'our pupil-teachers got more first class marks than any other school in the district'.

Sometimes we learn a little about individual teachers: Alice Healey completed her three years and went to Lincoln Training College. Another glowing report was given in 1895, when it was said that 'no better work than Joseph Field, Louisa Horton and Ellen Adams could be wished for'. Two years later, Louisa Horton, having completed her apprenticeship, became an Assistant Mistress. In 1903 James Mathews took first place in the Archdeaconry Religious Examinations with two others also placed in the first class. In 1890 the death of Alfred Unitt was reported. He had been a leading treble in the choir who then became a pupil teacher. He subsequently went to college and then to teach in London, where he became head of a school in the East End. He died aged 31.

From the Inspector's reports we get glimpses of the curriculum. Religious Education included not only the Bible in general, the Creed and the Catechism, but knowledge of the Acts of the Apostles, The Journeys of Paul, The Christian Year and Private Prayer. The girls were criticised one year because their recitation of 'Gloria in Excelcis' was not quite perfect. Her Majesty's Inspectors looked at Dictation, the Copy Books, Composition, Recitation, Arithmetic, Singing, Spelling, Grammar and Geography. The Infants had Collective Lessons on Common Objects and Collective Lessons on Colour. Physical Activity was encouraged; the little ones had Bell Drill, and boys had the services of a Drill Sergeant. Girls had Drill Exercises, too, and it was hoped that the girls at the National Schools 'would be known in the street by their erect and graceful bearing'.

Sewing was regarded as being very important. In later years the girls were taught cookery, and the boys were able to have woodwork lessons at the Institute. Good manners and general behaviour were carefully watched.

Just as the church fabric required constant restoration, so the schools needed money for enlargement and repair. The most pressing job in 1881 was to make more places available at the School in Alcester Road, and the Vicar led the way with a very generous gift of £100 towards the new classroom. Over £500 was raised by donation and a huge bazaar was held at the Vicarage, opened by the Mayor. Concerts were held in the afternoon and evening. There was a lawn tennis tournament, and a livestock stall where dogs, cats, rabbits and poultry were for sale. One raffle caused 'great excitement' when it was drawn. The prize was a portrait in oils of the Vicar by Mrs Fortescue. This event raised £318, and cleared the debt.

The completed classroom was opened by the Marquis and Marchioness of Hertford, who gained instant popularity by asking for a day's holiday, which was granted. Whenever there was a new extension, or if classrooms had been decorated, the Vicar asked notable people to view the result, and also asked the parents to come along and see the alterations. He was well aware that the more interest the local people had in the school, the greater would be its success to withstand the competition from the new Board School. Many parents felt loyal to the National School since they themselves had been pupils. They were also very familiar with the building because it was used for social functions in the town.

Some of the schools' income depended on government grants, and these were given in direct ratio to attendance figures, therefore good attendance was of vital importance. For example the grant to Alcester Road in 1903 was £796 18*s*. 0*d*. which included a special grant for cookery and £15 for pupil teachers.

The school at Shottery earned £66 12*s*. 0*d*.

The Vicar was much concerned about absenteeism, not only because it meant a drop in income, but also because he disapproved of truancy, and of parents keeping older children, particularly girls, at home, to act as 'mothers' helps' in families. Even when the school-leaving age was attained, he did not approve of boys leaving school without a job to go to, or girls being sent away in service, at the age of twelve. He felt the work of the attendance officer, who rounded up the absentees, was very important.

As usual, Arbuthnot tackled the problem in a practical way. He promised cards, prizes and, later, medals, to all those who could claim to be 'never absent, never late' each year. Since these awards were not given for scholastic achievement, everyone could become a prize-winner. The presentation became one of the annual events of the school year, usually awarded by the Mayor, or by one of the ladies from one of the local leading families – the Flowers or the Hodgsons. On one occasion when the Vicar's sister-in-law distributed the prizes, the Medals were 'handed to the happy recipients by his little niece, aged two and a half years, who was perched upon a chair, and performed the ceremony most gracefully'.

The Vicar always paid tribute to the mothers as well as to the scholars who were so regular. He was aware of the sacrifices some of the families made to pay for their children, and to get them to school regularly and on time.

This particular prize day in 1883 also shows us the important place of needlework in the girls' department.

> The following is the list of the awards for sewing made by a Committee of Ladies, to whom, as well as the Donors, all connected with the school are much indebted:
>
> Darning – Prizes given by Captain Arbuthnot, R.N. and Mrs Scarlett: 1. Leah Smith; 2, Mary Field.

Marking – Given by Mrs Arbuthnot and the Vicar: 1, Elizabeth Barnacle; 2, Amy Harris.

Button-holing – Given by the Vicar and Mrs F. Smith: 1, Annie Hirons; 2, Lucy Fisher.

Print Patching – Given by Mrs Kendall and Mrs Hutchings: 1, Ellen Taylor; 2, Ada Tompkins.

Linen Patching – Given by Miss Fenn and Mrs Hill: 1, Hannah Field; 2, Mabel Bagley.

Flannel Patching – Given by Miss M. Minet: Clara Beckett.

Gussets – Given by Mr Humphries and Mrs Parkhouse: 1, Emily Hopkins; 2, Harriett Wiggett.

Calico Garments – Given by Mrs Ashwin, Mrs Nason, Mr and Mrs Kendall and Mrs Bryan: 1, Kate Adkins; 2, Lily Fisher; 3, Louisa Bennett; 4, Anne Hunt.

Flannel Petticoat – Given by Mrs Nason: Elizabeth Hemming.

Knitting Woollen Stocking – given by Mrs North: Mary Talbot.

Knitting Cotton Stocking – Given by Mrs Nason: Emily Reeves.

Junior Room

Petticoat – Given by the Vicar and Miss McGriger: 1, Helen Badger; 2, Ada Gibbs.

Holland Apron – Given by Mrs Newland and Miss Oldaker: 1, Esther Cooper; 2, Faith Harris.

Pinafore – Given by Miss North: Alice Bradshaw.

Knitting Socks – Given by Miss McGregor and Miss Fenn: 1, Jane Birch; 2, Lilian Eborall.

No girl was allowed to take more than one prize, but the Vicar gave extra rewards to those two who obtained the most commendations. They turned out to be Leah Smith and Ellen Taylor.

The same year, 31 Scripture Examination certificates were presented, but the Vicar took 38 scholars – boys and girls – to Worcester to receive their awards. He did this every year. The prizes were often presented by the High Sheriff in the presence of the Bishop. The Vicar knew that the occasion would be valued as well as the prize.

In 1884 he was proud that Stratford children carried off more prizes 'than those from any other Parish in the Diocese – good for the teachers as well as the children'.

Books were favourite gifts though the Vicar often gave Penny Bank Books including one or two shillings to found a Savings Account. To scholars who already had a book he added a proportionate amount.

In 1884 one irate mother, Mrs Goode, took her two daughters away from the school and sent them to the Board School, 'because they did not get prizes'.

'Handsome' writing cases and work boxes were also popular; even a cotton frock and a silver thimble were given, and most exotic, presented by the Vicar, silk scarves from Damascus.

In 1901 Marie Corelli personally presented all the boys and girls with a new sixpence each, and all the infants with a new threepenny bit as a New Year's Gift. She also hosted a Christmas Party at the Memorial Theatre one Christmas for the Infants, with a huge Christmas Tree.

Possibly the most troublesome prize was that offered by Mrs Hodgson in 1885 for cleanliness and tidiness in the Boys' School. There were so many who could qualify, that the rules were modified to take in 'the never absent, never late' medal-winners. Three boys had received these medals four years running, but John Simms had been given a Bishop's prize at Worcester three years running and had never failed to pass all subjects at the annual examinations by Her Majesty's Inspectors, so he was deemed to be the Deserving Boy and was given a handsomely bound English Dictionary.

Several scholars achieved medals for six consecutive years – the whole of their school lives – and these were usually rewarded with half a guinea each from the Vicar. One exceptional girl stayed on at school until she was sixteen and gained eight medals. The Mayor added another half sovereign on this occasion.

A very popular 'prize' was the granting of a half holiday. These were requested after prize-givings sometimes. Mrs A. D. Flower not only asked for a holiday but invited the children up to The Hill, the Flowers' large residence near the Welcome Estate. Captain Holt inspected Drill in the Vicar's field. He expressed himself pleased and asked for a half-holiday, 'which naturally produced some hearty cheering'.

On September 23rd 1896 one was given because Queen Victoria had beaten the record by the length of her reign. The National Anthem was sung before the school broke up, but none could get further than the first verse.

In 1901 evidence was given of the splendid work the school was doing. Mr Tomline, Her Majesty's Inspector, was so pleased with the progress that HE asked for a holiday. 'We do not remember such a mark of approval on the part of Her Majesty's Inspector ever having been given since the new plan of inspection has been in practice' was the proud entry in the magazine.

Unfortunately, education was sometimes interrupted by epidemics of measles and scarlet fever. When the schools were closed, Sunday Schools also had to stop. Naturally examination standards were affected if the closure was for any length of time. The decisions were questioned sometimes. In 1894, after 25 children (out of 725) were affected by measles the step was regretted because it was only calculated to create a panic in the town. 'As long as children play together in the streets, it seems unnecessary to stop their assembling at school. We have heard of a case of a child, kept away from School on account of measles, taking part in the performances at the Theatre, which shows how impossible it is to isolate infected households.'

Arbuthnot's involvement with local education was enormous. He was, as Vicar, the ex officio Chairman of the Managers of Alcester Road and Shottery Schools, and for twenty-nine years served on the School Board of the Board School. Again, for most of these, he acted as Chairman. He was also a Governor of the Grammar School. For several years, with Mr Priest, he ran the Choir School, described in the chapter on 'Choirs and Bells' and later on, he was the driving force behind establishing the Church Institute. He made several efforts to run evening classes, and advocated the use of libraries and reading rooms – indeed, the Church supplied these until the opening of the Public Library in Henley Street. He also very actively supported the Industrial Training Home for Girls. He campaigned for a recreation ground and a safe area in which to swim in the Avon. He allowed endless cricket and football games on his field, and dancing on his lawn, recognizing that young people need to keep active. He arranged many lectures about foreign lands and famous people, illustrated by magic lantern slides. Some part of Sunday School and Band of Hope outings was usually devoted to improving the mind, though he maintained that even the experience of a train journey or trip on a boat down the Severn was educational to youngsters who had little opportunity for travel.

He urged parents to allow their children to stay at School as long as possible. In his address to parents at a prize-giving in 1889, he pointed out to them what a ladder was provided for a clever boy to climb. There were three Annual Scholarships offered at the Grammar School, and from there there was an annual Scholarship to one of the Universities, so that it might be said that a boy at the National School had a University degree within his reach. He was sorry there was not the same chance for girls.

By 1905 new rules and regulations were causing more problems for the Church Schools. The Vicar wrote of the new Educational Act,

> Its effect seems to diminish the authority of the local managers who, being on the spot, ought to know more about the requirements of the School, and to increase the rates by such needless extravagance as making our Pupil Teachers travel daily to Warwick, instead of receiving their instruction here. Surely, if it was advisable to send a candidate for two years to a Secondary School, which I greatly doubt, the Grammar School here is every bit as good as the King's School at Warwick. The result, as far as I am concerned, will be that I shall not want to employ any more Pupil Teachers when the present supply is exhausted.

Mr Arbuthnot never allowed anyone to be in doubt about his opinions. Two were repeated at frequent intervals in articles and sermons every year. Firstly, all Anglicans should have access to Church of England Religious Education, and secondly, it was unfair that rates paid by Church of England ratepayers should fund secular schools, when they already supported their own institutions.

He encouraged cleanliness, neatness, modesty, thrift and respect, and urged young people to avoid lying, bad language, idleness, smoking and drink.

Mostly, Arbuthnot was very vigorous and positive, but in the February issue at the beginning of the twentieth Century, on the same page that recorded the death of Queen Victoria, he seemed rather tired. He was, in fact, only fifty-five years of age but his health was not good. Changes were taking place, and he felt the old values were disappearing. He wrote,

> It appears to me that the effects of school training in afterlife are not so apparent as they used to be. Hooliganism is a lately coined word, to express roughness and rudeness on the part of young lads in public. I am not prepared to admit that Hooliganism exists in Stratford, but the conduct of some youths is not so decorous and self-restrained as it ought to be. There is not that respect for authority, that chivalrous politeness to women, that abstaining from wanton mischief, which I should like to see . . . But it is not only among Boys that the want of respect for authority is shewn. Ten years ago no girl in the National School would have thought of passing her Vicar in the street without a curtsy, now many do not notice me at all,

> and many who do, greet me with a nod which is suggestive of one of those Japanese dolls with loose heads. Of course, this does me no harm. It only saves me the trouble of acknowledging the greeting. But it is the sign of the times, and a sign which is not reassuring. We are not the only people who are lamenting the neglect of the 'Duties' of Christians, as taught in the Catechism. It is wide-spread over the country, and it is difficult to see any chance of improvement. The root of it exists in the absence of parental control. Most boys and girls are permitted to do just what they like at home.

Sometimes he must have looked back with regret to his first year in Stratford when it was written of the pupils at a School treat that there was 'pleasing behaviour – although merry and gay, there was nothing rude or rough in their conduct which must have been a source of gratification to their teachers'.

Chapter 9

THE SUNDAY SCHOOL

One of George Arbuthnot's main concerns was the Sunday School, and he worked hard to increase the numbers of scholars and staff, and to get the support of the parents. From a sermon which he preached in 1889, and which was published in the magazine, we can get some idea of size of the undertaking.

> Every Sunday in this Parish the following places are open for the instruction, not only of children but of those who are growing up to manhood and womanhood. The Parish Room, where a lay member of the Church instructs some twenty young men in the Church's faith, for three-quarters-of-an-hour before Matins. A room engaged in Chapel Street, where one of the Clergy has a morning class of younger lads. The Business Room at the Vicarage, where a layman has a class of still younger boys. The Room of the Choir School, where the Master of that School gathers as many of his scholars as will come to give them definite Church Teaching. All three Departments of the National School – Boys, Girls, and Infants – where two, and often three of the Clergy, including myself, are present, with about fifty lay helpers, at a quarter-to-ten, to teach some 500 children. When we look across the fields to Shottery, we find the school there open at the same time, and under similar regulations. And when we come to think of the afternoon, not only do we see this Church about three-quarters filled with children to listen to half-an-hour's instruction from their Parish Priest, after taking part in a bright and attractive Service, but also we find the Business Room at the Vicarage filled with a gathering of some twenty young women to receive teaching from an older person of their own sex. I have sketched out to you this manifold work, because I do think that the Clergy and Laity who carry it on, have some claim on your sympathy and support. And I look for this from different people in different ways. First of all, Parents may show their sympathy and give their support by sending their children to us. Let no foolish pride keep away those of higher social grade – no equally foolish pride detain those whose clothes are not so nice as their wearers might desire. Let no laziness or indifference make the children late in the morning. We find it needful for the discipline of the Schools to prevent scholars coming in after prayers, when the teaching has begun; but if Parents will take care, no child need be locked out. Oh let us not be pained any more by groups of children waiting in the playground, when they ought to be in their places within! And again, I want to ask all parents, whether they go to the Sunday School in the morning or not, to make a point of sending them to the afternoon Service. I should like to see this Church filled end to end on a Sunday afternoon with young people and children. There is no reason why this should not be. I almost always speak to

them myself, and I value more than I can tell this opportunity. I do not care to see children coming to the evening Services, unless indeed they come with their parents – but I do want to gather all the young of the flock of every class in the afternoon, and if any older ones will come with them, I venture to think they will not always fail to hear and learn something they did not know before. Parents, will you try to bear this in mind – that we invite every child in the Parish, from three years old to sixteen, to come here on Sunday afternoon?

No wonder that he was always asking for more teachers and more funds, and that he should say on one occasion, just before he went on holiday, that he found Sunday School work more exhausting than the Church Services.

Times and venues varied, but for thirty years, classes to suit every age group were provided. During his first ten years, over eight hundred youngsters attended. After that, numbers declined, but were rarely below seven hundred since to the Sunday School Roll were added the special classes. The Vicar even ran a class on Friday afternoons to teach the Catechism and the Book of Common Prayer to children educated at home or in a private school. Frank Smith also taught a similar class.

It was not easy to recruit as many teachers as he needed. All the Clergy took part as a matter of course, and he had a core of dedicated, capable workers on whom he could rely, but always more were sought.

Each teacher received a card of instructions:

The School opens in the Morning at 9.45 and in the Afternoon at 2.30 and teachers are requested to be *REGULAR* and *PUNCTUAL* in their attendance.

If they are unable to be present they are requested to intimate the same to the Superintendent, and to provide a substitute if possible, subject to his approval.

Teachers' meetings are held fortnightly, at which their attendance is very earnestly desired, but whether present or not they are expected to *PREPARE BEFOREHAND* and to *TEACH* the lesson appointed for that day.

Teachers are recommended to visit the Homes of their Pupils and always to call when a child has been absent more than one Sunday. They should endeavour to enlist the parents' sympathies in their work.

They must remember that their work is a religious one, and can only prosper if it receives God's blessing. With this object they should themselves be regular Communicants, and make their children and their teaching the subject of daily prayer.

A special Celebration of Holy Communion will be held in the Parish Church every year, on St Nicholas' Day, December 6th at 8 o'clock at which all Teachers are invited to be present, and to make the School the special object of their Intercession.

A special prayer was printed on the card for use in private devotions.

The Archdeaconry of Worcester held an Annual Meeting of Sunday School Teachers to which Stratford teachers were encouraged to attend. In 1896 it was held at Holy Trinity.

Arbuthnot was very keen that teachers should visit their pupils' homes. He said, 'A good visiting teacher will always have a well-filled class.' He also encouraged teachers to support each other, and a social gathering was held every year either after Communion on December 6th or on an evening near that date.

As usual, the great problem was to raise money to fund this activity. Althoug all teachers were volunteers and, indeed, paid half of the cost of their teachin notes themselves, there were other expenses to be met. Rooms had to be heate in winter, other teaching aids were needed, and Sunday School prizes had to b bought.

Treats and parties were funded separately.

Preparation classes were not always well supported, the teachers most in nee of assistance often being the poorest attenders. In June 1901 another method o help was tried.

> In order to avoid mistakes we propose to give the subject of the lesson for each Sunday in the month, so that the Teachers may prepare it from their book of Notes, and the children may know what they are to be taught. We add also the questions from the blue books to which the answers must be repeated and we remind Scholars that if they do not learn the appointed lesson, they have no right to expect to go on the Summer Excursion.
>
> June 2nd The Cities of Refuge
> 9th Theocracy
> 16th Ruth
> 23rd Samuel the Prophet
> 30th Saul the King
>
> Questions
>
> June 9th Which are the two great Sacraments? What is a Sacrament? Who ordained the Sacraments?
>
> June 16th How many parts are there in a Sacrament? What is the outward sign in Baptism? What is the Sacred or holy thing which is conveyed by it?
>
> June 23rd Is the Holy Spirit given to all who receive the Sacrament of Baptism worthily? How do we receive the Sacrament of Baptism worthily? Why, then, are Infants, who cannot have repentance and faith, baptised?
>
> June 30th Are Infants too young to be brought to God in Baptism? What was the first promise which our Godparents made for us in Baptism? What was the second promise?

We do not know the age group for which these lessons were intended, but thi sample gives us a flavour of the kind of instruction which was given. Those wh learnt their lessons and answered well could gain Reward Cards. These were give to the scholars who had obtained the highest marks in their classes for the month Nine cards entitled the holder to a First Prize Book, and six cards gained a Secon Prize Book. Small Prayer Books, Church Service Books, and Reference Bible were most often given.

Occasionally there were additional treats. One year, when an Annual Outin for the whole Sunday School had to be abandoned for lack of funds, the Vica entertained all the prize winners to tea at the Vicarage – 58 boys one day and 6 girls the next. Each party was entertained by a Magic Lantern Show. Another year all scholars who had gained 90 marks out of 100 between September 1st an Christmas were invited to a special party. Edgar Flower gave a Christmas Tree an a Conjuror provided the Entertainment.

Scholars also entered the Bishop's Examination of Religious Knowledge.

For some years the Collect for the Day was learnt by heart, but the practice was dropped, though children were expected to remember certain texts. Learning by heart was not completely abandoned.

In 1903 the Vicar offered 5/- to any child who could recite The Sermon on the Mount without a single mistake. Three claimed the prize money. He offered a further sum the following year to any who could memorise John chapters XIV, XV, XVI and XVII. Five girls tried, but none succeeded. However, in view of their excellent attempts Arbuthnot awarded one girl 3/6 and the others 2/6 each.

After the Parish Parlour was built, the large afternoon service was split into two. The older children went to the Church, and the Infant classes went to the Parlour. It was felt that it was difficult to interest all the groups with so wide an age range. The children of Shottery had a similar service every month.

Helpers, as well as teachers, were needed to 'help the little ones to find their places' – and to keep order.

Men teachers were always in short supply; some of the 'strong sex' were needed, since the 'fair sex greatly preponderate'. In one issue there is an appeal for a lady to take a Bible Class for girls in her own home on Sunday Mornings at 10 o'clock.

In Summer time the fortnightly preparation class took place in the Church on Wednesdays after 8 p.m. Evensong.

Special children's services were held in Advent and Lent. Anyone absent from Good Friday Service was automatically disqualified from the Summer Excursion. A strict register of attendance was kept to keep track of those who were eligible for Christmas Parties. Only genuine illness was accepted as an excuse. Sometimes an outbreak of scarlet fever or measles could completely close the schools and cause the cancellation of Treats, though a substitute was arranged when things got back to normal. In an attempt to protect children from smallpox, after 1903, children who had not been vaccinated were refused admission to the Sunday School.

The children were encouraged to take an interest in the wider work of the Church. During the period of restoration they collected pennies to pay for the Children's Window by the North Porch and on one Sunday each month their collection supported a rescued slave girl, Anne Hathaway Kalunda, at a Mission School in Zanzibar. The children sent gifts as well as raising the money.

The Sunday School was also used as the venue where lessons of thrift, so dear to the heart of George Arbuthnot, could be learnt. A clothing club – a means of saving for winter clothes and boots – was well established. It was open to all Parishioners who had need of it, irrespective of religious Creed. There was also a Juvenile branch connected with the Sunday School. Any number of children in a family could buy a card for a penny and enter small sums each week. Regular saving was encouraged by adding a bonus for the number of deposits rather than on larger amounts entered at intervals. Any child who saved a penny a week for a month, had an extra penny added to his total. At the end of a year another shilling was added as a bonus. Later the bonus was raised by another ninepence to three shillings a year. Although the Post Office paid some interest, the good people of Stratford rallied round yet again and contributed to the Bonus Fund.

The Vicar always sought close co-operation with parents asking them to senc their children regularly and in good time. children who were late were excludec after prayers had started, thus losing valuable attendance marks from the total needed for the Treats. He also asked that parents should listen to their childrer repeat the lessons they had learnt in class.

Most of all, parents must remember their obligation to present their sons anc daughters for Confirmation. The Vicar disliked accepting candidates under 1 years, and tried to raise the age to 14. Some drifted away from Sunday Schoo when they left their Day School, and many left when they had been confirmed.

Arbuthnot was a realist who knew that the scholastic level of some candidate was very low, but he thought they should be able to say the Creed and the Lord' Prayer 'fairly well'. The better educated should know the Catechism. Mistresse with maidservants of Confirmation age were urged to grant the girls the facility o attending preparation classes. Because of the diversity of candidates, some still a school and many out at work, five or six preparation classes were held each yea on a variety of days, and at different times and venues. For example, in 1902 lad and young men met on Sunday mornings at 9.45 in the Parish Parlour. Anothe class for boys was held at St James' on Thursday evenings at 8.00 p.m. whicl followed a meeting for girls and young women at 7 p.m. The Business Room a the Vicarage was used on Thursdays at 4.15 and again on Friday at 8 p.m. It wa hoped that every candidate would find an appropriate meeting. A further class wa arranged for adults.

After Confirmation great efforts were made to encourage the youngsters tc become regular communicants. Organisations like the Girls Friendly Society anc the Church Lad's Brigade, helped to attract this age group, and keep them activ members of the Church Community.

Chapter 10

'WELFARE STATE'

. . . those things which are requisite and necessary as well as for the body as the soul.

– *Book of Common Prayer*

At the end of the nineteenth century the poor and sick still looked to the Church and the wealthy for help. George Arbuthnot took his charitable responsibilities very seriously. The Church in Stratford naturally administered the older established charities like Tasker's, and Newland's, and Lady Conway's at Luddington. Candidates for certain alms houses applied to the Vicar. On rare occasions a vacancy in the Leycester Hospital in Warwick was advertised in the Parish Magazine.

Dr Collis had introduced 'lady visitors' to the Parish before Arbuthnot arrived, and he extended this method of welfare work with enthusiasm. Miss Lawrence was appointed in February 1880 as a 'Mission Woman' and soon she had a large team of helpers. It was emphasised that the ladies were church workers and not relieving officers. They were called The Guild of District Visitors (D.V.s) and to each was assigned an area of the Town. They were to report all cases of sickness, and spiritual or temporal distress. Urgent cases were given immediate attention; others, less pressing, were discussed at monthly meetings with the Vicar. They were to endeavour to bring all families to attend Church, and their children to Sunday School. They were also to give information about all parochial clubs and charities.

Poverty and sickness could be alleviated by gifts of tickets to be exchanged at local shops for goods. Relief was never given without investigation and money was *never* given. Visitors were also expected to read to the sick and aged. Their ministry extended to Dissenters as well as to members of the Church of England. The Vicar stressed that no one was refused aid from the Benevolent Fund on religious grounds. Many nonconformists gave generously for the work.

The ladies were asked to remember all, especially the ungrateful and rude, frequently in their prayers. They should avoid the temptation of putting the temporal before the spiritual, and they must never have favourites. Among other duties, they collected Clothing Club subscriptions and sold the Parish Magazines. The Church had a supply of blankets which were lent out to poor families every winter. Gradually the D.V.s took on the job of distributing these. Every spring they had to be returned after having been washed. Sometimes the demand was so great that those who had had loans the previous year had to be refused. When the stock was replenished, old blankets were sold off very cheaply.

Margaret Arbuthnot
(By permission of The Shakespeare Birthplace Trust, Stratford-upon-Avon.)

The ladies also lent out the 'Maternity Bags'. These contained bed linen and baby clothes, and were a great asset to poor families. This service appears to have been offered to Church of England families only.

This specimen form of application was printed in 1880.

MATERNITY BAGS

These are kept at the Vicarage for use in the Parish, and lent under the following conditions:

1. The recipient must be a respectable married woman who has resided at least one year in the Parish.
2. Her children, if old enough, must attend the National Schools, Alcester Road, and the Church Sunday School.
3. The baby must be brought to Holy Baptism at the Parish Church or St James' within two months of its birth.
4. The contents of the bag must be washed and returned in good condition within five weeks.

I recommend Mrs .... of .... for a bag, and believe she will fulfil the above rules.

This paper must be brought to the Vicarage at least one month before the bag is required.

The District Visitors met every year for a special Celebration of the Holy Communion on the Feast of St Martin.

Ladies in the Parish who were involved in the work included Mrs Arbuthnot, who regularly visited one of the poorer streets in the town.

The Clothing Club was well supported. Subscriptions to this useful fund were collected by the District Visitors or paid by children in the Sunday School. The Club was open to parishioners without regard for religious differences, though in 1903 a warning was given that no woman was to be admitted to the Club 'who had not sought God's blessing on her marriage either in church or chapel, or one who refuses to bring her children to be baptised, or declines to allow them to be vaccinated.'

Approximately five hundred pounds was collected every year, and to this was added a bonus given by benefactors. All money was given back in tickets to be spent in local shops. The tradesmen also gave a discount, so Club members got very good value. The Coal Club was run in a similar way. Five hundred and eleven townsfolk saved for fuel in 1903. The total was £415 5*s*. 1*d*. to which was added a bonus. Most years soup kitchens were held. In 1881 one was open three days a week which provided a better service because bread was served as well as soup. That winter, an average of one hundred and twenty children were served with a breakfast of tea, bread and butter in the Vicarage classroom. The previous year over a period of sixty-eight days, four thousand, four hundred and sixty breakfasts were served. The Vicar wrote 'many children who must have been famished have been kept in health and several honest, striving families have been enabled to reduce their weekly bread bill through the late hard times.'

The Mothers' Union proved a popular institution. Members would listen to a 'suitable talk, usually about family matters, and have a cup of tea'. Arbuthnot knew the importance of domestic competence in the home. He once wrote: 'The inability to cook on the part of working men's wives has driven many a man to the public house.'

A typical meeting in 1905 began with a prayer and a hymn; then Mrs Mason from Warwick gave a 'simple' address urging all mothers to instil good habits into their children, and have the courage to root out all the bad ones. 'Swearing, smoking (for grown lads), overdressing, and lying were the special faults she touched on.' A 'Capital' tea was thoroughly appreciated, and 'Miss Winnie Hewer charmed all by singing some songs'. The collection at that meeting amounted to 11*s*. 0*d*. (55p).

For many girls domestic service was the only work available. This often meant leaving home at thirteen or fourteen to live with strangers. There might be little social contact with employers and life could be very lonely. The Girls' Friendly Society offered an opportunity for girls to meet together where they would be in no danger of mixing with 'low company'. Only single girls were eligible to join.

The objects of the Society were:

1. To bind together Associates and Members, for mutual help, for sympathy and for prayer.
2. To encourage purity of life, dutifulness to parents, faithfulness to employers and thrift.
3. To provide the privileges of the Society for its members wherever they may be by giving them an introduction from one Branch to another.

Locally, various ladies of wealth and influence added prestige to the movement. With the members, they attended an annual Event. This was usually a lecture followed by tea on the lawn of a patron's house. Then everyone would go to the Church for the annual service.

On one occasion they were addressed by Mrs Townsend of Honington Hall, the foundress of the Society. Mrs Fortescue of Alveston Manor was secretary for a time and the Marchioness of Hertford, who was president for some years, opened a Home of Rest for members, near Ragley Hall.

After her marriage to the Vicar, Mrs Arbuthnot became an enthusiastic worker and supporter. Her group met regularly, and did needlework which was sold to swell their funds. They had talks and prepared little plays and concerts. Most years an excursion was arranged. The girls were encouraged to save, and sometimes long service awards were given.

To any girls leaving school for other situations, the following advice was given:

> It would be well, before you leave home, to call on your Vicar, and ask him to give you a letter of recommendation to the clergyman where you are going. And then you will find that you are not treated as a stranger; and however lonely and dreary you may be for a time, you will feel that you have a home in God's House, a friend in God's priest, and the same blessed and comforting ordinances you have always enjoyed.

One particularly interesting experiment in social work was situated in a house near Holy Trinity:

> An important addition has been made to the Charitable Institutions of Stratford by the opening of an Industrial Training Home for girls. The object of this Institution is to provide education and suitable training for domestic service for workhouse children, and other destitute girls. Children who have been brought up in the workhouse have little experience in household matters, and, in consequence, make very incapable servants, and often have to be sent back to what is their only home. It is to be hoped that this Institution will give girls the experience of training they cannot get in the workhouse. Lady Hertford is the Patroness, Mrs Starkey, the Lady Superintendent, and it is managed by a committee of ladies. The Vicar is the Chaplain, the Priest-Chaplain the Treasurer and Mr Nason the Honorary Medical Attendant. An efficient Matron has been secured; and it was opened for the reception of inmates on Friday, May 11th, with a short prayer, said by Rev. F. Smith, after which the Marquis of Hertford declared it open, and expressed his hearty wishes for its success.

The Home was situated in College Street and functioned for many years. The girls made useful garments which were sold to support the Institution, and occasionally 'pound days' were held when well-wishers donated packets of foodstuffs – sugar and garden produce – to help with the housekeeping.*

Domestic servants were not the only work people for whom the Vicar showed concern. He visited all the shops in the town personally, in order to establish one early closing day each week. The shopkeepers were only prepared to close if everyone agreed. For the assistants it was a great concession. He then tried to introduce a further reform. In 1898 he wrote, 'A vast improvement has taken place in the hours during which Shop Assistants have to work. But we think there is still room for improvement in one respect. Many of the shops keep late hours on Saturday. Some do not close until 10, and this entails the assistants remaining till 10.30 or 11. Even the errand boys are kept late on Saturdays. If this were unavoidable nothing more could be said. But it would be quite easy to do away with this hardship, if only the chief tradespeople would agree on united action. Let all announce, especially the grocers, that they will close sharp at 9, or at 8.30, and the persons interested will soon learn to do their shopping before then. We commend this matter to those whom it concerns, and can assure them that whoever takes the first step in the direction of closing at an earlier hour on Saturday will earn the gratitude, not only of the assistants, but of many fathers and mothers in this town.'

He also asked shopkeepers to provide chairs for shopgirls who were on their feet for so much of the day.

In 1890, he pointed out to small dress-making establishments in the town that the Factory Act applied to them as well as the large clothing factories, and that apprentices should not work more than sixty hours a week.

---

* Mrs Beryl Smith, who died in 2004 at the age of 102, remembered some of the girls. They dressed in blue-grey frocks with white aprons and were always 'well turned out'. Part of their sewing project included making three sets of underwear each so that they were equipped to go into service.

In 1900 the following notice was printed.

A WARNING

> The Clergy of England have been asked to warn young women in their Parishes against accepting situations in Paris in connection with the Exhibition to be held there this year. Anyone doing so, and going there without most careful previous enquiry, will run great risk of finding herself in a dangerous position.

The Education Act of 1872 provided the opportunity for young people to lear
to read. Many clergymen were anxious that 'wholesome' literature of a goo
moral tone should be available to meet the needs of this newly created market.
Stratford curate, the Rev. W. K. W. Chafy-Chafy had promoted a Pure Literatur
Guild in 1872 as a branch of the Stratford Church Workers Association. By 188
there were some seven or eight-hundred volumes which could be borrowed b
subscribers paying a penny per month. The Guild employed the 'Guild Hawker'
who visited the homes of the poor and offered for sale high class serial literature
coloured pictures and texts, wallpapers, pamphlets, sanitary and other tracts. I
eight years he sold 31,949 articles. George Arbuthnot wrote, 'Most of the home
of the labouring classes are in some degree adorned by objects supplied throug
the Guild, whilst the direct and indirect influence of its "pure literature" mus
have produced considerable fruit.'

When the hawker left in 1885 his work was continued by the District Visitors
Temperance pamphlets were distributed and sold along with publications lik
'The British Workwoman', 'Sunshine' and 'The Gospel Missionary'. The librar
books were housed in several different venues over the years and various hours o
opening were advertised in the Parish Magazines. Finally, in the February editio
of 1906, after the Free Library in Henley Street had been opened, the followin
announcement was published:

> A matter of general interest to the Parish has been the opening of a Free Library secured for us by the generosity of Mr Carnegie, and the persevering exertions of a few patriotic citizens. It has proved a great success, and the number of books taken out has exceeded all expectations. If a large proportion of these are of a light character, we must remember that novel reading diverts the mind, and kindles the imagination, and so is not unhealthy in moderation, and we may feel sure that the Library Committee will exclude from its shelves all books of an immoral or baneful tone. As this Library seems to cover all the ground, I have felt justified in disposing of the old Parish Library, which has served its purpose in the past, but was no longer needed.

The money raised by the sale was soon earmarked for another project.

Arbuthnot wrote, 'A free library is an excellent thing for the older member o
the community, and so is a Technical School, but young blood needs to let of
steam by some athletic process and for this purpose nothing is better than
gymnasium.' In 1905 he was able to lease a large building in Tyler Street whic
had rooms suitable for many activities, by which he hoped to attract young me
away from public houses. This was called 'The Church Institute'. Once again h
appealed for money. He needed £36 each year for the rent and a further £10 to £2

for fitting up the rooms. The gymnasium equipment was bought at The Army and Navy Stores with the money raised by selling the Church Library.

At the end of the first year he was able to report that the Church Lads' Brigade used the largest room for drill as well as gymnastics. It was available one evening a week to any lad in the town who paid six pence (2.5p) a month. This fee paid for the services of an instructor.

The C.L.B. and the Temperance Society made use of other rooms, one of which was equipped with a bagatelle board. Another was supplied with books and daily papers. Two further rooms were set aside for the use of the newly-formed Men's Social Club. Already fifty members had joined and they met every evening except Sunday. Plans were being made for a debating society and a cycling club. Rooms could be hired and the County Council rented one room for carpentry classes.

The health of the Parish caused him much concern. He was so keen on vaccination he even made it a provision for joining the Sunday School in 1903. He often emphasised the importance of clean hands and included an article on the care of the teeth, since 'the loss of the teeth is not only unsightly, but most productive of indigestion'.

He was a great advocate of exercise. On several excursions swimming in the sea or river formed part of the day's entertainment. He encouraged 'mixed' bathing as long as participants were decently dressed which meant that adolescent boys were to wear tops as well as drawers. Since he was called upon to bury the victims of several bathing fatalities, he was much concerned that the Town Council should provide a safe bathing area. 'Knowing something of the scarcity of baths in the town and the habits of the young' prompt action was needed. It was pointed out that it was perfectly legal to bathe in the river and to those who feared indecency, it was suggested that 'a custodian, strong, active and able to swim should be put in charge. If the man was armed with a good cane, no more would be heard of splashing passers-by or bad language.'

National schemes were under way for fresh water supplies and the disposal of sewage, but much remained to be done.

In 1906, the Vicar expressed his concern that villagers in Shottery were at risk, because sewage was draining into Shottery Brook. Compensation had already been claimed for injury to cattle.

Many homes in Stratford were poor and overcrowded. When a member of a family died it was difficult and distressing to keep the corpse in the house. Arbuthnot offered the bier house, on the south side of the Church, as a safe and undisturbed place for the coffin of any person who was to be buried according to the rites of the Church of England.

It concerned the Vicar that poor families would get into debt over funerals, so sometimes he would print the basic costs of various expenses, and was often generous in waiving all, or part of, the fees.

Self-sufficiency was much encouraged. The Vicar offered prizes at local flower shows for the best produce, and he advocated keeping poultry, rabbits and bees. To encourage young children to grow things, he gave away seedlings, and again he offered prizes for the best results. In November 1900, two thousand bedding plants were offered at the National School.

After twelve months in the Parish, he realised that Rural Poverty wa increasing. Machinery was replacing manpower on farms. So, in his desire t better conditions of the 'labouring classes', he advocated the possibility c emigration to the colonies. In 1882, he quoted a letter from the Archbishop c Canterbury to *The Times* saying that 200,000 British subjects had left the U.K. i the previous nine months to seek a new life. The Vicar wrote: 'Can Charity tak a better form than that of assisting men with families to seek a new home wher work is abundant? I shall be happy to obtain full information on the subject fo any who feel disposed to go.' He engaged C. Nevill-Rolfe, Esq., to speak o 'Emigration to Queensland', at Shottery and Stratford. The talk containe 'excellent advice', and pamphlets were available at the Vicarage.

Much of the money needed for social work came from wealthy parishioners The names of these generous benefactors recur over and over again supportin various Sunday School activities: the coal club, the bonuses for the clothing clul and, most importantly, the Benevolent Fund. The Vicar was unfailingl appreciative of their donations, but he also sincerely thanked those who gave smal amounts, the pennies and half-pennies, which he called 'The Power of the Littles'

Subscriptions were charged for certain activities but they were always ver modest. In 1880, use of the Parish Library cost a penny a month. Admissions t meetings were only two or three pence, and the price usually included a cup o tea.

Many, many concerts, plays, waxworks, service of songs, bazaars, fetes and sale of work, not only provided activity for various groups within the Church, but als raised a lot of money. Other things as well as money were required. Tradesme were asked to donate bones, sugar, semolina and vegetables, to provide 'penn dinners'. At other times the Vicar begged for books (not the goody, goody type) games, tables, chairs, sheets, blankets and other goods, especially children' clothes and boots.

The local hospital, the Nursing Hospital and Children's Hospital and th Provident Medical Institution, though not run by the Church, were wel supported by annual collections and sales of work. Donations were also made t worthy medical institutions, including Birmingham Eye Hospital and the Femal Refuge in Leamington.

For each guinea raised for Stratford Hospital, a ticket of admission wa obtained. For example, in 1881 one ticket kept a child in hospital for four weeks These tickets were issued by the Vicar, often on the advice of the District Visitors to deserving cases. He was always appealing for further tickets from rich friend who subscribed to the hospital privately.

Animal Welfare was not forgotten either.

This passage, from a sermon printed in a magazine, not only shows hi concern, but gives an example of his style of preaching. The address was based o the story of Abraham's shepherds digging wells for their cattle.

> Let me give a very practical turn to our thoughts, by suggesting some points in which the lesson seems to be called for. First, in regard to the keeping of pets, whether birds or beasts. I think the young require to be reminded of how dependent they are upon them for the supply of their needs. Food and water which they can

obtain for themselves when in a state of freedom, must be given them when in a state of captivity. I do not suggest that children will be wilfully cruel to a pet animal, but children are forgetful, and sometimes do not appreciate the sufferings of their pets, who have no means of making them known. Their rabbits, for instance, are too often unprovided with water, dogs are kept without exercise, birds are not given clean food, and in many similar details our pets are made to suffer. But if this chiefly concerns the young, I think my next point ought to touch all. Animals are given us for food – we are justified in slaughtering them for this purpose, but it must be done with as little suffering to them as possible. I am sure that many of my hearers must share the pain I often feel when I see unhappy sheep being driven up some narrow entry to the slaughter-house at the back of some butcher's shop. They are, I believe, keenly sensitive to the smell of blood, and the terror which they feel as they approach it is clearly shown in their desperate attempt to escape. I am not accusing anyone of intentional cruelty, when I proclaim my opinion that we ought to do away with these private shambles, and have a public slaughter-house outside the town where all the latest improvements can be introduced, and where everything will be under the constant supervision of an authorised inspector.

Thirdly, I am afraid that we cannot acquit some of these employed outside our sale grounds of unnecessary harshness in their handling of the cattle under their charge. I have seen acts which have made my blood boil, and I do not think our police are sufficiently alive to their duty in regard to this.

Christian teaching and high moral principles permeated all this social work. Arbuthnot attracted a good deal of criticism, but few could doubt that he genuinely wished nothing but good for his parishioners.

Chapter 11

MISSIONS

> We fear that many of our readers take little interest in Christian Missions, and are hardly alive to their duty in connection with them. Our Lord before His ascension commanded the Church to preach the Gospel to all nations, and that command is still addressed to us as the Successors of the early Christians. As we cannot in person carry it out, it is our duty to help those who do, both by our prayers and our alms. Probably all admit this in theory, but when asked to carry it into practice, they plead the great local demands made upon their purses, and point to the numbers in our own land who are as ignorant of God and Christ as any heathen far away. These, they say, have a prior claim on their interest and their money. But we should like to ask, where should we be now, had the Apostles acted on this principle? There were numbers who knew not Christ in Jerusalem and Palestine, but the Apostles did not all remain at home to teach them, or we might still be lying in heathen darkness. And following the Apostolic example the Church of England should endeavour not only to gather in the masses of heathen at home, but to convert also the heathen abroad.

George Arbuthnot showed his deep concern for missionary work in these words in 1882. At home, funds were raised annually for the 'Additional Curates Society' and 'Waifs and Strays'. Special services were arranged with visiting preachers and there were many appeals, collections and sales of work. Much of the money raised for the A.C.S. was by regular annual subscriptions from generous parishioners, but collecting boxes, for smaller amounts were available. Not all meetings were well attended. After one it was wryly observed, 'Unless you give them tea and cake it seems impossible to get Stratford people to an evening meeting.'

Contributions were also given to the Mission to Fishermen on the Deep Sea Fleet at Yarmouth.

Three Overseas Missions were supported, the Society for the Propagation of the Gospel, the Central African Mission, and the Madagascar Mission. Through the CAM, two children were adopted at the Mission School at Mbweni. It would seem that they were both rescued from slavery. In March 1892 this report was printed:

> News has been received from Zanzibar, that a little African Boy in the Mission School has been baptized under the name of William Shakespeare, and that his maintenance will be looked for from the fourteen Parishioners of Stratford who have promised to collect 10*s*. a year for that purpose. His surname is Mabruki. We trust

that William Shakespeare Mabruki will attain to the same eminence in Africa as our illustrious townsman.

The Scholars of the Sunday School have also determined to support a girl in the Mission School; and it is proposed that when she is ready for baptism, she should receive the name of Ann Hathaway, her surname being Kalunda.

Photographs of both these children are in the Vestry of the Parish Church, and will be shown to any who care to see them. The knowledge that they have a little girl, all their own, for whom £7 a year must be raised, should stimulate the Sunday Scholars to greater efforts on the monthly Missionary Sunday.

The progress of both the children was well reported in the magazine.

The following is the report just sent home of the progress of 'our girl', in her school. We trust it is considered satisfactory by her 'god parents' in Stratford.

Mbweni, November, 1882.

Name – Ann Hathaway Kalunda. Whence coming – H.M.S. Lodon. Supposed age – 8 years. When baptized – 10th April, 1882. Class and standing in School – Class VII, No. 5. 1. Reading – Very good. 2. Scripture – Good, answers well. 3. Writing – Fair. 4. Arithmetic – Fair. General character – Very intelligent, and an extremely nice thoughtful child. Progress since last report – Very good.

Three years later, we hear about her progress.

Reading – Good. Scripture – Good. Writing – Tolerable. Arithmetic – Good. General Character – Rather obstinant and very disinclined to submit to pupil teacher of her class. Truthful and a clever girl; on the whole a nice child. She was confirmed on St. Andrews Day and received her first communion at Christmas.

Apart from school reports, the Vicar's brother, Captain Arbuthnot, whose ship, H.M.S. Mariner, was stationed on the East Coast of Africa, sent further news. This extract written in May, 1889, shows that the Navy cooperated with the Missionaries.

I left Zanzibar on Sunday May 12th, bound for this part of the coast, which is about 200 miles to the Southward. Before commencing our blockading work I had got permission to take Bishop Smythies of the Universities Mission, and several others who were going up country with him, down as far as a place called Tunghi, whence he was starting on his annual tour of visits to their various stations in the interior. . . . He is a charming man and it was a great pleasure to have him on board for four days. He and a young clergyman who was accompanying him lived with me in my cabin. . . . He did an evening service for us, the Sunday he was on board, and preached a very nice sermon. . . . Just before leaving Zanzibar I had the honour of being introduced to Ann Hathaway. She is a fine strapping young woman, and is, I should say, a credit to the Parish that has fathered her; she seems also an intelligent girl, and is a great favourite of Miss Thackeray's, the principal lady in charge. She is engaged to be married to a young man, who is, I believe, a native teacher in their schools, and highly respectable, but Miss Thackeray is anxious that they should wait another six months, as the girl is young. I have not seen William Shakespeare, as he is gone out into the world, and is independent of the Mission, but I believe he is conducting himself well, and earning an honest livelihood as a mason. . . . I think it is time that the Parish should nominate two more godchildren.

Six months later Captain Arbuthnot wrote again:

October 23rd

Yesterday morning, early (7 a.m.) I went out to the Mission Station at Mbweni, in order to see the marriage of two of the girls there to two young men also connected with the Mission, one of them a native teacher from a station on the mainland, the other a carpenter in the town here. One of the brides was named after my predecessor in this ship 'Emma Durnford' having been taken in a slave dhow by him about four years ago. They (the brides) were very well got up in white dresses, with sort of muslin head-dresses and short veils behind; all the other girls in the school attended as bridesmaids. After the Marriage ceremony, the Holy Communion was administered, the service being very impressive. In the afternoon they gave a breakfast to about a 100 friends of the two brides and bridegrooms, but I could not stay to see that; one of the Vice-Consuls, who went out with me, took several photos of the bridal party, which will be rather interesting to keep. . . . Ann Hathaway will be married before long! I saw her young man yesterday, they say he is a very respectable lad, he has been a teacher up in the interior for about two years, and has now come down here to complete his education, with a view perhaps, if he turns out really well, to his being some day ordained. William Shakespeare, I am afraid, has not turned out so well, but I have not heard much about him lately.

In 1900 another rescued slave girl was baptized Judith Siwangine. She wa trained for laundry work. She was steady, well behaved, and took an interest i native basket work.

We learn of one other sponsored child – again rescued from slavery. Sh actually wrote to the Vicar. The letter, translated from Swahili, was printed in th Magazine.

A description of an African funeral was printed in 1885.

The following news has been received from Central Africa, and as it mentioned 'our boy', it will be read with interest by many who contribute to his support.

The chief event of the month was the death and burial of Sepindu, the Sub-Chief and Governor of Umba. It may be remembered that he was drawn to the mission by the Rev. C. Yorke, and both before and after his (Rev. C. Yorke's) death was very hearty in aiding the cause in every way. In 1879 he was elected Churchwarden of Umba. He seems to have died suddenly away from home. Mr Lowndes heard of his death at Kivindo, on the 10th, and that the body had been taken to Umba. Sepindu's boy, Charlie, had been treated successfully by Dr Petrie for spinal curvature, and Sepindu himself had been under his care, but had left Magila on hearing of a relative's illness, and his own death seems to have been unexpected. Mr Lowndes writes:

'I heard at the market that Sepindu had died, and soon after my return received a note from John Swedi asking me to go at once to take the funeral. So I at once despatched Josiah, the schoolmaster, to send Ackworth Songolo after us, and took our four biggest boys – Gainsborough, Walter, Welford and Henry, and also Peter and William Shakespeare, as choir, with a change of clothes, and some food in their hands. We set off just as the mid-day bell rang. We walked at a good pace and arrived there at 2.30. They were waiting for us, and we had hardly time to wash our hands and put ourselves in order before the firing of guns and the loud wailing of the mourners told us that the procession had started. John Swedi began the service. I read the lesson at his request. On leaving the Church we sang "Brother now thy toils are over", which lasted till we reached the grave. Old Semkali, the chief, was near us in a clean white kausu. The boys sang well, but the loud wailing must have drowned it, except for those near at hand. John Swedi took the service at the grave. We then returned singing the hymn "Jesus lives", and as there was less noise I trust that something of it was heard. There must have been present several hundreds of heathen friends and relatives, and comparatively only a handful of Christians, and the wailing and almost howling were heathenish and horrible. I am very glad that no attempt at any of the heathen burial rites was made. It would not have been right to delay the funeral, otherwise both Mr Wallis (who came over from M'Kusi) and Ackworth would have been present, as they arrived soon afterwards. I was very glad we had all gone over, not only for Sepindu's sake, but I think the old chief Semkali and his people were pleased with the mark of respect. He was present at the evening service. Sepindu is laid by the side of Charles York.'

The writer is the son of a Worcestershire clergyman, who has left his home to carry the Gospel to Africa. Such letters as his make one feel the reality of Mission work.

It is interesting to note how English practices were imposed on African culture – the school reports, the dress of the brides, the election of Churchwardens, and the choir at the funeral singing hymns that would be familiar to a Stratford congregation.

Mrs Arbuthnot took a particular interest in a school run by the Assyrian Mission. For this she raised £4 a year chiefly by subscription. Regular reports arrived. In 1898 we learn that the school was in a village called Mushabad and it was attended by 27 pupils, all girls. They were examined in reading the New Testament in Syriac and reciting the Lord's Prayer, the Creed and the Ten Commandments. All could do some mental Arithmetic, and eight knew the multiplication tables. The elder girls were 'fair' in spelling, but the younger ones were 'weak'. A few could write, though not well, on slates; several had learnt texts by heart, and all knew simple prayers. . . . The sisters pronounced the needlework good.

Although the Central African Mission was the centre of much of the interest in overseas work, many speakers came to tell of their experiences in other parts of the world, often showing pictures of the areas where they had worked. The Rev. W. B. Wright came from Japan, others came from India, Burma and China. The Rev. E. F. Lipscombe spoke about work in the North West of Canada, the Rev. Walter Beck spoke on two occasions on North America and the Rev. J. F. Teakle came from New Zealand. Some got V.I.P. treatment. When the Archbishop of Calcutta spoke in the Town Hall, the Marquis of Hertford took the chair, and the Vicar entertained many a Bishop. In 1897 the following notice appeared:

The duty of churchmen to support Missions both at home and abroad, will be brought before the Parishioners this month. The Bishop of Zanzibar, the successor of the saintly Bishop Smythies, is going to spend Monday, 16th, at the Vicarage, and the Vicar is issuing invitations to an 'al fresco' Tea that evening, at which the Bishop will give some account of his work. Missionary Boxholders will be specially invited, and asked to bring their boxes to be emptied and returned. The Vicar will be happy to see any whom he may have accidentally overlooked in sending out the cards. The Bishop will celebrate at the Parish Church on Tuesday morning.

The tea was attended by 200 people.

That year a Conference was held at Lambeth and a good number of Bishops found their way to Stratford. Although, of course, no appeal was made for missionary work in the States, I am sure Arbuthnot was delighted to welcome so many representatives of the world-wide Church. He wrote:

The strong sympathy that exists between the Church in America and the Church in this country has been strikingly demonstrated by the visits that have been paid to us, in this year of the Lambeth Conference, by Prelates from across the Atlantic. The Bishops of New York, Minnesota, Georgia, Cairo, Washington, North Carolina, and California have all preached in our Church, and besides them, the Bishops of Iowa, Pittsburgh, and Wyoming have been here.

Later it was reported that the Bishop of Colorado preached an 'excellent' sermon, the Bishop of Kansas came for the day, but the Bishop of Pennsylvania was 'obliged to give up his promised visit'.

News was given of anyone with local connections working as a missionary. The Rev. Maude's sister-in-law was stationed at Bloemfontein Mission and a school friend of Arbuthnot was Bishop there. In a letter from the Archdeacon of Kimberley, information was received about a former chorister at St James'. His name was Edgar Rose and he was the son of a veterinary surgeon in Stratford. He first helped as a layman but later became ordained. He was invited to preach at Holy Trinity and give a lecture on his work. Two curates went to work in India and we can be sure that their careers were followed with great interest.

To support the work, money was chiefly needed. The main method was by individual collection boxes placed with families. About 100 were used, but they were not all in individual homes, the G.F.S. Sewing Class, The Industrial Home for Girls and various Sunday School Classes contributed too. Usually a great 'Opening' was held at a special meeting and each amount was recorded in the magazine. Many contained very little cash – the box for Shottery Choir in 1902 produced 1*d*. – but although everyone was urged to give more, the Vicar was truly appreciative of all that was given. He published the following advice:

Say a prayer silently when you put your money in: 'O God, accept this for Christ's sake.' You will then always remember that you are giving to God.

The box is further useful to receive thank-offerings for special mercies, e.g. You get good news from a distant friend – put the value of the stamp which brings it into your box; a child has a shilling given it – put one penny into the box, etc.

Boxes ought not to be used for begging. We have heard with regret, of little children ringing doorbells, and asking for money for their box. We hope they will never get any that way.

Boxes ought not to be used to receive coppers which we want to get rid of, such as French pennies.

The 'adopted' children were mostly supported by Sunday School children who undertook to raise 10/- each, every year. Their efforts were augmented by Sunday School collections. Boxes were distributed to households for Home Missions, too.

Parcels of clothing were made up. We are told of regular 'working parties' held at the Vicarage followed by sales of work in aid of mission funds. Sometimes a lady would lend her drawing room for such an event. Rarely a month passed without some function to raise money being advertised or reported in the magazine.

Three publications – *The Mission Field*, *Central Africa* and *The Net* – were widely circulated in the Parish.

Chapter 12

THE TEMPERANCE MOVEMENT

George Arbuthnot's work in Stratford on behalf of the Temperance Movement became one of his most relentless crusades. In the first issue of the Magazine he wrote:

> Our two greatest enemies in improving the temporal, as well as the spiritual condition of our people, are Drunkenness and Improvidence. The former we try to combat by the Church of England Temperance Society, conducted on the truly Christian and liberal principle of admitting on equal footing, those who abstain altogether from intoxicating drinks and those who use them in strict moderation.

He had two aims. The first was that by exhortation and example his parishioners might be dissuaded from the use of alcohol, and the second was that he hoped to provide alternative, wholesome entertainment in place of the warmth and convivial society offered by the public houses.

At a later date he wrote, 'Man is a gregarious animal – he likes society – and the Public House gives a working man the society of his acquaintances, after working hours. There are many who have wives and young families and very limited accommodation at home. It seems to me small blame to them if they do not care to spend the whole evening there.'

Having recognised the problem, in a very practical way, he sought to make other entertainments just as attractive.

Already in the same first issue he declared, 'I do not see why we should not try to open a Coffee Palace and a Club or Place of Rendezvous for Working Men.'

Immediately steps were taken to establish a Stratford Branch of the Church of England Temperance Society (C.E.T.S.). In February 1880 a public meeting was convened. The Vicar took the chair. The speaker was the Rev. W. Kipling Cox, the Diocesan Secretary, who subsequently came many times to Stratford Meetings. It was reported, 'There was a fair attendance, but there were not so many of the upper classes present as we should like to have seen. We fear some over zealous Temperance Workers have alarmed them, and led them to confuse Temperance and Total Abstinence, and to think that the Church Society is to be composed of none but reformed inebriants.'

Three forms of pledge were available to would-be members:

1. I hereby agree to abstain from the use of Alcoholic Liquors, except for Religious purposes, or under Medical Order.
2. I hereby agree to abstain from the use of Alcoholic Liquors, except at my meals,

or when taken for Religious purposes, or under Medical Orders.

3. I acknowledge my duty as a Christian to exert myself for the suppression of Intemperance, and having hereby become a member of this Society, will do my utmost, both by example and effort, to promote its objects.

Those taking the second or third pledges were deemed to be equal members with those taking the first.

The following suggestions were made as means by which the last promise could be carried out.

> By never giving drink for work done, or in lieu of money – by resisting the present system of treating in business transactions, and the footing custom among workmen – by promoting every counteracting agency, such as Working Men's Clubs – and by discouraging the payment of wages, and the meeting of Benefit or Friendly Clubs at Public Houses.

The movement grew quickly from sixty-four members in 1881, to one hundred and fifty-five in 1882, to two hundred and eighty-eight in 1883.

The Coffee House

In 1881 a business proposition to establish a Coffee House was launched. A thousand pounds worth of one pound shares were offered for sale, though only half the money was needed at the outset. The committee was made up of the Vicar, the Rev. F. Smith, Mr Nason, Mr Newton, Mr Norris, Mr Eaves, Mr Winter and Mr Deer. The building was quickly fitted out, though the town council expressed a fear that gambling might take place on the premises! The Parish Magazine queried the potential of dominoes and bagatelle as games of hazard. The Enterprise was called 'The Coffee Palace' and it was officially opened by the Marquis of Hertford on 23rd November 1881, at a special meeting at the Town Hall. The Vicar made a speech in which he said that 'the promoters had no desire to display hostility to the publicans. They wished to enter into friendly rivalry with them. If the former had the right to sell beer, the Company had an equal right to sell tea and coffee. 'Live and let live', was their motto. The assembly, led by the Marquis, walked from the Town Hall to The Coffee Palace where everyone drank to its success in a cup of coffee.

The Palace played an important role in the temperance movement in the town for many years. As well as promoting non-alcoholic drinks, it also sold food and did 'outside catering', often providing teas for Sunday School Treats and other functions.

Some entertainment, in the form of 'penny readings' took place on the premises, but one of its main activities was to host an Annual Friendly Society which met alternate Mondays. Five years after its inception it was reported:

> The Temperance Annual Dividend or Benefit Society, of which Mr Norris is Secretary, continues to do good work. I invite all who wish to belong to such a society to join it rather than one held in a Public House. I often wonder how a clever English workman can be taken in by these Public House Benefit Clubs. They are held entirely in the interests of the landlord, who by their means not only attracts

custom to his house, but also has a hold on his customers to ensure payment of their debt to him; and then at the end of the year manages to secure a good part of the dividend by having a Supper! I hope most of my Readers can see through such a very shallow trick. I believe if it were not for their Clubs many Public Houses might as well be shut up at once.

True to his belief that it is no use depriving people of one source o entertainment without providing another, the Vicar arranged a series o 'entertaining' evenings, for the burgeoning C.E.T.S. At first, members met every two weeks, but the meetings became so popular that they took place every week These were held in the National School. They were free to members. Visitors were charged tuppence. A cup of tea and a piece of cake were always served Children paid sixpence, the high charge was made to discourage youngsters since they had their own Band of Hope activities. Mostly, members provided their own entertainment with songs, monologues and readings. Chorus singing was much enjoyed. When later, the Parish Parlour became the venue, 'Pops at the Parlour was held every Saturday night.

There, for the modest sum of one penny, our youths can spend a pleasant evening listening to music and song, which will send them home happier, healthier and wealthier than an evening spent at a Public House can do.

After the regular Winter sessions, soirees and garden parties took place on the Vicarage lawn. The C.E.T.S. also formed a cricket club, playing in the Vicar's field Not all concerts were performed by members. On Shrove Tuesday and Boxing Day fund-raising events were usually held.

This is a typical programme:

The C.E.T.S. Entertainment given at the National Schools on Boxing Night, proved to be a great success. By the appointed time, the Room, which had been prettily decorated with flags, banners, evergreens, was well filled by an audience numbering upwards of two hundred. The programme was opened with a well-executed overture, 'Waldandacht', played by Miss A. Harris, which was followed by a song, 'True till death', by Mr E. Weston. The trio, 'A little Farm', was then sung by Messrs Jarrett, who secured an encore; after which a violin solo was beautifully rendered by Miss M. Hunt. Mr Keating next sang 'Love's request', which narrowly escaped an encore. 'Cherry ripe' was then sweetly sung by Miss Large. Miss Harris displayed a further proof of her skill in the pianoforte solo 'Herzeleid', which was followed by a song from Miss Hunt, 'Whisper and I shall hear', with violin accompaniment by her sister. Mr Keating again appeared on the boards and rendered 'A Soldier and a Man' in fine style. The audience now showed their high appreciation of Miss McNeille's musical talent by demanding a well deserved encore of her song, 'Pierrot'. Miss M. Hunt again favoured them with a violin solo, 'Grossmitterchen', and the song 'Anchored', by Mr Weston, brought the musical part to a close. After a short interval, the dialogue, 'Drunk and sober', was performed by Messrs F. & H. Clayton, S. Field, T. Hollick and E. Jarrett, in a manner that reflected credit both on the performers and Mr Norris, whose untiring energy in preparing them must have been rewarded by the hearty applause given by those present. Mr E. F. Parker, who had accompanied the songs during the evening, then played 'God Save the Queen', and brought a thoroughly enjoyable evening to a close.

Miss Hodgson from Clopton House sometimes organised an event to raise funds. One was a 'Café Chantant', she was assisted by Miss Charlotte Arbuthnot. Alongside the entertainment promoted by the C.E.T.S. there were many serious lectures. Some were by speakers specially invited to preach at rallies. Others formed part of a series of talks. Mr R. Lydgate, F.R.G.S. gave four talks in 1889. Two of his subjects were 'Alcohol fails to promote health or afford nourishment to the body, illustrated by chemical experiments' and 'Arctic Exploration with Nansen, showing work by Abstainers, illustrated by limelight views'. On another occasion, Mr Tweedie from London demonstrated 'the uselessness of alcohol as food'. Rev. W. Kipling Cox, on one of his many visits propounded 'the economical argument'. Mr Langston, the Temperance Missioner at Winson Green Prison spoke.

He related some of his experience with the prisoners who are daily discharged from the prison, and to whom he tries to give a fresh start in life, and he declared that the very great majority of them had fallen into crime through strong drink.

The Rev. T. S. de Courcy Laffan, the headmaster of King Edward's School, preached at an Open Air Rally. Mr Mark Knowles, a celebrated Temperance lecturer came to talk about his life and 'his own rise from being a workhouse boy, to a barrister at law'. Admission was free but alas attendance was poor. 'The wet night was one cause . . . but the apathy of the people on the subject of temperance was a greater.'

When the Dean of Hereford, the Honourable and Very Reverend James W. Leigh addressed a meeting in the Town Hall, it was said that he was well known as a 'stalwart abstainer' as well as 'our Lord Lieutenant's brother'. The Vicar never failed to indulge in a little 'name dropping' in order to help the cause. Several articles by notable supporters of the movement, appearing in the national press, were reported in the magazine. The Archbishop of Canterbury was frequently quoted.

Readers were reminded that Queen Victoria was a Patron of the C.E.T.S. and the Band of Hope. She had received the Chief Khama of Bechuana and his entourage and it was reported that she had said, 'I approve of the provision excluding strong drink from their country. I feel strongly on this matter and am glad to see that their Chiefs have determined to keep so great a curse from their people.' Most pleasing, however, to the temperance workers, must have been the following item from the *Birmingham Post* in 1901.

TOASTS

When people think of it the custom of drinking toasts is very absurd, but, like other absurd things, it has a strong hold on the public, and is not likely ever to be abolished. We have therefore read with great satisfaction the subjoined paragraph in the *Birmingham Post* of July 16th –

DRINKING THE KING'S HEALTH

The *Daily Telegraph* this morning says: 'A naval officer wrote to King Edward asking if he could issue an order that his Majesty did not consider it necessary that, when his health was given, it should be drunk in wine. The King's Secretary replied that his Majesty thought the Lords of the Admiralty would not like his interference by issuing orders, but he would be glad if it was circulated privately that his Majesty considered that his health was as much honoured by those who drank it in water as by those who drank it in wine.'

Although Arbuthnot regarded the work of the C.E.T.S. as important, his rea concern was with the young people of the Parish, so a Band of Hope was formec to help children establish habits of abstinence in their early years. He urged:

all Parents to allow their children to join the Society, and we add a few of the Rules that they may judge for themselves: No Member is admitted without the Parent's consent in writing. Every Member, on admission, pays 2*d.* for a Card and the Rules, and a Subscription of one half-penny a Month, due at the first meeting in every Month – this Subscription entitles each Member to a Monthly Temperance Magazine.

Every Member on admission solemnly makes the following promise: 'I promise to abstain entirely from the use of all Intoxicating Drinks, except under medical order or for religious purposes, as long as I remain a Member of this Society; and if I break this promise I will immediately own it to one of the Officers of the Society.' The Boys also promise to abstain from Tobacco.

One of the first projects was to form a Drum and Fife Band. They were trainec by Rev. G. H. Moor. Several concerts were held to raise funds for instrument and, eventually, uniforms. The Band accounts printed here were published jus before a Sale of Work by which it was hoped to clear the debt.

As was stated in last month's Magazine, the proceeds of the Sale will be devoted to paying off the debts of the Drum and Fife Band of the Society, the accounts of which we give below. Should any balance remain after this debt is paid it will be devoted entirely to the Band of Hope. Many things are wanted; perhaps the most pressing need being uniforms for the band boys. Neither theatrical losses, nor the handsome banner, lately purchased, will be paid for by this Sale of Work. The former is borne by the promoter of the theatricals, and the money for the latter was all collected by Mr Baily at the time of purchase. It is well to mention this to correct mistaken ideas on the subject, which seem very common. Many of the trade of this town have very kindly sent articles from their shops to help the Sale, and perhaps others, who have not thought of it, might do the same. Cut flowers, and flowers in pots, for purposes of decoration are much wanted. All contributions should be sent as soon as possible to the Rev. G. H. Moor, 16 College Street, who will be very grateful for all help.

The following are the Band accounts from the starting of the Band two years ago to the present date.

	£	s.	d.		£	s.	d.
To Band Boys' Subscriptions				By Riviere & Hawkes for			
to Nov. 1881	2	5	0	Side Drums and Fifes	4	12	10
To Band Boys' Subscriptions				" Bass Drum	4	9	6
from Nov. to August, 1882	1	18	2	" Carriage of Drums	0	3	0
" Fee for Playing at G.F.S.		10	0	" Fifes	2	5	0
				" Drum heads	0	4	2
				" Tenor Drum	2	12	6
				" Three side drums &c	4	10	6
				" Cymbals	1	8	0
				" Triangle	0	1	0
				" Gas for 1880–1	2	0	0
				" Lessons	4	19	6
				" Three Boy's Time	0	1	10
	£4	13	2				
Deficit	22	14	8				
	£27	7	10		£27	7	10

It must have been a proud moment on Whit Monday in 1883 when they turned out in their uniform for the first time. They marched down to the Town Cricket Ground and played lively airs at intervals during the afternoon. The general verdict was 'very favourable both as regards the appearance of the lads and their playing.' Thereafter they played on every possible occasion. Later, when a trainer was needed, he was required 'not only to teach but keep order'.

By 1883 there were four hundred and twenty members in the Band of Hope including a small branch at Shottery. A very active programme was arranged. There was singing and dancing on the Vicarage lawn. Many concerts were prepared of songs, recitations and little plays. Some activities were mixed but often boys and girls met separately. In summer the boys played cricket on the Vicar's field and in winter the girls had a sewing group.

Mrs Arbuthnot became a very enthusiastic worker with the girls. She organised 'Service of Songs'. One was called 'Chubby George'. A little play called 'The Flower Queen' was performed and she took the cast to Broadway Tower as a treat. They were conveyed there in a large break* and, after spending a happy afternoon, returned by moonlight. Their production of 'Carnival' had to be postponed because of the death of Queen Victoria.

We read of cycle rides, a fireworks display, ping-pong tournaments, 'sumptuous' teas, sports' days and preparations for the competitions held at Diocesan Rallies. Mrs Arbuthnot's Girls Choir featured largely on these occasions.

Not all was enjoyment, members were expected to enter the Diocesan Temperance Examinations. These were taken very seriously. In 1901 the subject was 'The History of the Temperance Movement in England' and as part of the preparation a magic lantern lecture was given. Results were eagerly awaited and

* A break (or brake) was a horse drawn vehicle.

there was great rejoicing when the Silver Challenge Shield was won. In 1902 i
was put on display in Mr Eccles' window for all to see.

George Arbuthnot's attitude to the Annual Mop Fair was typical. He deplore
the drunkenness, the indecency of some of the peep shows, and the fact tha
much-needed house-keeping money was wasted by poor families, but, because h
was powerless to stop it, and it was a much-loved institution, he did what he coul
to raise the standard. The Coffee House and the Corn Exchange became centre
where non-alcoholic drinks could be bought at reasonable prices and where th
fair-goers could have a rest. He encouraged his clergy and congregation to atten
the event and report any stall showing lewd material to the police, and he not onl
attended himself but took distinguished visitors with him. We are told that th
Very Reverend, the Dean of Winchester, while visiting Stratford to preach at
Harvest Festival, 'showed his genial character by taking part in some of th
amusements of the Mop'.

In 1900 another means of spreading the work of the Temperance Society cam
to Stratford and the following notice appeared in the Magazine:

> One of the Temperance Vans sent round the country by the C.E.T.S. will be located in this Parish from the 27th of this month to the 3rd of September. Two speakers will accompany the Van, and outdoor meetings will be held each night. We hope that some interest will be stirred up in Temperance Work. No charge is made by the Society for the visit of this Van, but hospitality is required for Men and Horse. The Vicar has undertaken to keep the horse for the week and he will be glad to hear from any kind friends who may be willing to give two nights hospitality to the men. It is intended that they shall be two nights at Shottery, two at Luddington, and the rest of the week in Stratford. Anyone who is willing to take one or both of them in for two nights is requested to communicate with the Vicar, or with Mr Davis, the Hon. Sec. of the local Society. They will be content with quite humble accommodation.

Occasionally the magazine printed recipes for non-alcoholic drinks. Th
following were suggested in 1889:

DRINKS FOR THE THIRSTY

Some people get thirsty in this hot weather, especially when working hard, and some are foolish enough to think they must drink beer to quench thirst. We believe that anyone of the drinks of which we give recipes will be found much better than intoxicants, and we ask a trial of them especially in the Harvest Field.

Stokos is prepared thus: Put from three to four ounces of fresh oatmeal, ground as fine as flour, into a pan, mix with a little cold water to the substance of cream, then add five or six ounces of loaf sugar, and a fresh lemon cut in thin slices with the pips taken out. Add a gallon of boiling water. Stir thoroughly while the water is being poured on. Use hot, warm, or cold. The lemon may be omitted or any other flavouring used instead, half ounce of ginger (bruised) per gallon may be used if preferred. Cost 3*d*. a gallon, or five gallons for 1*s*.; four lemons are enough for five gallons.

Cokos is a good nourishing drink, made as follows: 4 oz. of fresh fine ground oatmeal, 4 oz. of cocoa, into a pan mixed with a little cold water into a thin batter then add 6 oz. of sugar, pour on a gallon of boiling water (stir while water is being added); take to the field in a stone jar. Cost 4*d*. a gallon.

Hopkos is a good harvest drink: Boil half an ounce of hops, and half an ounce of ginger (bruised) in one and a half gallons of water for twenty-five minutes; add 1 lb of best brown sugar, and boil ten minutes more, then strain, and bottle or put into a cask while hot; it will be ready for drinking when cold. It should be kept in a cold place. Dried horehound may be used instead of hops. Cost 3*d*. per gallon. No yeast must be used in making Hopkos.

Once, it printed a sentimental story (in two parts) by Mrs Laffan, the wife of the headmaster at King Edward's School. The story had a happy ending when the hero signed the pledge and was reunited with his sweetheart.

Probably the most exciting functions of the C.E.T.S. and the Band of Hope were the excursions and the big rallies. Places like Bournemouth and Portsmouth were chosen and on one occasion they went to Burnham by train and from there by boat to Cardiff. The children also went to local venues like Alveston and Hatton Rock.

The big rallies meant joining with other branches and going to hear speakers of national reputation. These were stirring events. The first, and probably the most outstanding, was at the Crystal Palace in 1882. One hundred and fifty-four Stratfordians left at 5.30 a.m. (accompanied by the Drum and Fife Band) and returned home again at 1.00 a.m. the following morning. The Vicar wrote with great satisfaction, 'I fancy that a few years ago a special train run by a Temperance Society from Warwickshire to the Crystal Palace would have been an impossibility.' He was delighted. As the Stratford Branch grew they attended the local annual festivals and joined in many of the competitions. This report appeared in 1896.

The Annual Festival of Diocesan Branches of C.E.T.S. was held at Moseley Botanical Gardens on June 27th, and was attended by a considerable number from our parochial branch. The President and Mrs Arbuthnot and Mr Weston, the Honorary Secretary, were of the party and over 120 members of the different juvenile organisations. The Festival was a striking and successful demonstration, over 1,000 juvenile and 500 adult members being present from all parts of the Diocese. Much interest was taken in the Athletic sports, and we are glad to say Stratford gave a good account of itself, S. Righton winning the Sack Race, and G. Goode the Wardrobe Race, while Winifred Edge ran 2nd in the Girls' Race, and C. Hygate and Righton ran a dead heat in the Three-legged Race, though in running it off they lost. There was a Singing Competition for a Challenge Banner, and hopes were entertained that Mrs Arbuthnot's Choir, which won it last year, would retain it, but greatly to the astonishment of most people, the judges awarded it to a Choir from S. Mark's, Leamington. Of course, nobody thinks of disputing with the judges' decision, though they may disagree with it, and our Choir contents itself with this quotation:

'Tis not in mortals to command success,
But we'll do more, Sempronius, we'll deserve it.

In 1901 an important development took place. A rally was held at Welcombe o[f] all the Temperance groups in Stratford. The clergy had worked together in thei[r] opposition to the way in which certain licences were granted and now they mad[e] a very public demonstration of their common cause.

TEMPERANCE FETE

The Temperance Fete, which we announced in our last number, took place on Saturday, August 24th, and favoured by beautiful weather proved a great success. It was chiefly memorable for two things. First, it brought together Temperance Workers, of all varieties of religious views, showing that in the battle with drink soldiers who wear different uniforms can stand shoulder to shoulder – and secondly, it was a proof to all who saw the procession as it moved down our principal streets that the Temperance Party in this borough are by no means to be despised. We do not affirm all present were Total Abstainers, but all were friends of Temperance, and all the Juveniles at least were Teetotallers. Of these there were about 300, and of the Seniors nearly 400, who sat down to Tea, besides many who came after tea. The general Rally was, very appropriately, at the Fountain in Rother Street, where the two mounted Marshals, Mr J. Henson and Mr H. Sankey, took command. In the procession the Banner of the C.E.T.S. followed immediately after the Town Band*, escorted by a detachment of the Vicar's J.A.U., and the Boys' Band of Hope, with blue scarves and wearing the Badge of the Society. Immediately behind walked the Vicar, and the two Clerical Speakers, the Rev. W. A. Baker-Beall of the Worcester Branch and the Rev. H. Sergeant of the S. Alban's Branch of C.E.T.S. These were attended by H. Coles as an Aide-de-camp on his Bicycle, and were followed by a small contingent from Shottery. Behind came the Girls of the Band of Hope, under the command of Mrs Arbuthnot, making an imposing display, with numbers of bannerettes of blue and white, and many of them wearing blue sashes. The Shottery Girls marched behind these, and some Senior Members. A representative corps from Snitterfield followed, and then the Baptists mustered in force, with the Rev. F. Watts and Mrs Watts in charge. A large body of Wesleyans, wearing blue rosettes, with Women of the Total Abstainers' Union, formed the rear guard, headed by the Rev. T. and Mrs Angold, Mrs Mansell, and other Leaders of the cause, prominent among whom was Miss Wright, who afterwards delivered an admirable Address. At different parts of this great procession we noticed Mr C. C. Davis, the C.E.T.S. Secretary, who contributed greatly to the success of the day, Mr Weston, the former Secretary, still keen in the work, and Messrs Norris, Hughes, Byrd, Inns, Gibbs and others wearing a blue and white rosette denoting that they were Stewards of the Fete. Lady Trevelyan had kindly placed Welcombe at the disposal of the Fete Committee, and a more suitable place could not be found for such a gathering or, we must add, a more amiable and courteous gentleman than Mr G. R. Deer who represented her and, with those who worked under him, laid the party under immense obligations.

At 3 o'clock a large Meeting was held on the Lawn, at which three short pithy speeches were delivered, and some Temperance songs sung. Then came tea for the

---

* The National School Cadet Corps took over the Band from the Band of Hope in 1900. Marie Corel[li] generously helped the Vicar pay for new uniforms.

Juniors, to the number of 300, and after that for the Seniors, numbering nearly 400. Here occurred the only *contre-temps*, as the planks provided for seating some of the party proved unequal to their weight, and the Temperance folk found themselves where they do not often lie, *on the ground*. Happily no serious injury was caused, and every one took the accident good humouredly.

After tea came the Sports, which lasted until such a late hour that the prize-giving was rather confusedly carried out in the gloom, and it was quite dark before the party returned to Stratford.

Similar events took place at Welcombe and Clopton over the following years. Arbuthnot greatly appreciated the support of the Nonconformists. In 1905 he even advertised one of their meetings in the Parish Magazine. He wrote, 'If we do not make much progress here in Temperance work, it has at least this to recommend it, that it draws together many who, as Churchmen and Nonconformists, have no other common platform, and I am glad to take this opportunity of thanking my brethren of the Nonconformist Ministry for the helpful way in which they have co-operated with me in keeping this great question before our fellow-townsmen.'

Within the Church, George Arbuthnot could promote temperance work through the C.E.T.S. and the Band of Hope, but he took his fight against drink beyond the welfare of his congregation. He frequently bemoaned a lack of support. In 1883 he wrote that 'there is still a vast amount of prejudice among the upper classes against the Temperance work which we cannot understand, though we feel its unfortunate effect'.

In another issue he showed his concern by stating, 'The source of much of our poverty and nearly all our crime . . . I believe to be drink.' He continued:

I do not say Drunkenness, but Drink, and I ask you to observe the difference. It is Drink which directly or indirectly produces many of the deaths which occur – I appeal to the Doctors if this is not true. It is Drink which is at the bottom of almost every crime brought before the Magistrates – I appeal to the police if this is not true. It is Drink which is the cause of nearly all the poverty and want, and rags and wretchedness, which makes our hearts bleed – I appeal to those who visit among the poor if this is not true. And yet we have constant evidence that those who are in authority, and those who occupy our high places, have as yet failed to realise this truth. This Town is practically making no struggle against Drink, and the few who have espoused the Temperance cause meet with neither sympathy nor support.

He deplored the giving of alcohol as presents and 'treating' friends in pubs. He also objected to giving bottles of drink as prizes. The following item appeared in 1896:

While on the subject of Temperance we cannot omit to call attention to the unfortunate revival of the practice of giving wine and spirits as prizes to the Volunteers for good shooting. This year's prize list included 6 bottles of whisky, 4 of sherry, 8 of port, a case of spirits, and 27 gallons of beer. It is in no spirit of hostility to our gallant citizen soldiers that we comment on this, and we give full credit for kind intentions to the friends who presented the prizes, but we must say that we do not think it the right way to encourage good shooting. Fancy a man shooting well, who was in the habit of steadying himself with a nip of brandy!

One great cause of concern to the Vicar was the serving of alcohol to the inmates of the Workhouse. He queried that any ratepayers' money should be spent on liquor and he was against beer being served as a 'treat' on Christmas Day. In 1895 the vote against beer for the festivities was nearly carried. The Chairman finally voted against the motion. He admitted, however, that at the Christmas Dinner some inmates took too much beer. The Vicar was not pleased. 'Thus we have the announcement on the highest authority that some inmates of our Workhouse observed the Birthday of Our Saviour by getting drunk, with the permission of the Guardians. We trust that this will speedily lead to some reform.'

The following year, for the first time, beer was forbidden on condition that the Vicar gave each man two ounces of tobacco and each woman some tea and sugar. Those Guardians who had not been present for the vote passed another resolution at the next meeting, that beer should be served on the Feast of Epiphany. The Vicar, who had already spent £3. 14*s*. 0*d*. on tobacco and tea, was justifiably cross. A clerical member of the Board had said that there was no breach of faith because the beer was not given on Christmas Day.

Arbuthnot delivered a roll call of those who drank water with their Christmas plum pudding: the Archbishop of Canterbury, seven other Bishops, two of the five Parish Clergy, all the Non-Conformist Ministers of the Town and most of the Head Teachers. He reminded the Board that many paupers arrived at the Workhouse because of their former immoderate use of beer – it was wrong to revive an old taste. He spoke of other workhouses which had banned drink. He was pleased to report that all the Clerical Guardians 'except one who ratted' voted against beer. The clergyman turned out to be the Vicar of Ullenhall who was aggrieved by the term 'ratted'. The Vicar apologised saying that he 'never meant to impute dishonourable motives to the gentleman', but added that it did not do for clergymen to be too thin-skinned.

The annual granting of licences to houses was a regular cause for complaint. First, there were too many and secondly, three belonged to the Corporation. The Vicar did not think it suitable that the rate-payers should own pubs. He disapproved of back doors down side streets and objected to a 'snug back room . . . where cab-drivers, waiting at the birthplace, might refresh themselves free from observation.' He was scathing about the magistrates granting a licence to the new Stratford Hydro, before any capital was subscribed for the building, and he was concerned that the brewing companies, who owned some of the pubs, put pressure on the tenants to sell more than they should. He criticised some of the sentencing. In 1899 the following item was copied from the *Herald*.

DRUNKENNESS

Stratford Police Court, Oct. 9th. Present: The Mayor, Messrs R. M. Bird, and R. I. Greene, Magistrates: 'W.S.' of Shakespeare Street, was charged with drunkenness in the streets. He was found lying asleep in the street at 12.30 in the morning, having mistaken the outside of his house for the inside, or not having been able to find his own door. The majority – *mark that word majority* – of the Magistrates dismissed the case. Have the same gentlemen ever sent a wretched tramp for seven days hard labour for 'sleeping out' under a hedgerow or in a barn?

It was not mentioned where Mr W.S. got the drink, nor does the *Herald* say any questions were asked.

The last question was very often asked by the Vicar.

There has been an unusual number of persons before the Borough magistrates lately, for the crime of drunkenness, or others springing out of it. We were glad to read in one case that the Mayor indicated the possibility of imprisonment without the option of a fine. We congratulate the police on their activity, but where are the persons who served these drunkards with the drink? Why are they not in the dock? We know it is very difficult to get a conviction in such cases, but we think the attempt should be made.

and again:

The report also stated that 29 tramps, or pea-pickers, had been convicted of drunkenness in July, but it did not state where they got their liquor. That is a question which the police ought to be able to answer. Tramps are not likely to carry about a large supply, so it must have been purchased somewhere. The Magistrates depend too much upon the report instead of seeing for themselves.

In 1899, together with the clergy of other denominations in the town, the Vicar presented the following Memorial to the Licensing magistrates at the Brewster Sessions.

THE MINISTERS' MEMORIAL

To the Worshipful the Mayor and the Magistrates of the Stratford-on-Avon Bench.

We, the undersigned Ministers of the gospel, residing in this Borough, respectfully approach you on the occasion of your holding the annual Court for the issue of licences for the sale of intoxicating drinks.

We represent congregations who differ in outward forms of worship, but we are all united in the desire to advance the cause of temperance in the community. To this end, we would ask your attention to the report of the Licensing Commission which has been presented since your last meeting, and point out that although no legislation has yet resulted therefrom many of the reforms suggested can be inaugurated without it, if those who are responsible for the administration of the law, as it now stands, will fearlessly do their duty. It is within the power of your honourable bench to inspect the agreements between the tenants of tied houses and their landlords, and when a transfer is applied for to examine the transferer on oath as to his reason for surrendering his charge. It is also incumbent, we venture to suggest, upon licensing justices personally to inspect the premises they license, and to satisfy themselves as to their suitability for the trade.

As residents in Stratford-on-Avon anxious to maintain the honour of the town, we feel bound to call attention to the disgraceful scenes witnessed in our streets on Bank Holidays, and to the fact that the police seemed quite unable to put a stop to them, and we would ask how it is that so very few cases of permitting drunkenness on licensed premises or serving drunken customers, are brought before the magistrates?

We are aware that the serving of children under 16 with intoxicating drink is not forbidden by the law, but we believe that an expression of opinion from the Bench that this practice is highly undesirable would receive the attention it deserves from all publicans who wish to conduct their business in a satisfactory manner.

The number of licensed houses in the borough appears to us to be far in excess of our requirements, but as long as the police have no complaints against any of them we do not suppose that any reduction will be made. But we think that some of them require careful police supervision, and we hope that your honourable bench will give such encouragement to our police as will lead them to do their duty in this respect. – We are, your faithful servants, George Arbuthnot, W. M. Armistead, F. C. Watts, E. T. Allen, Francis Smith, E. N. Dew, H. J. Gully, Herbert Wilson.

The Vicar and other members of the deputation wished to address the Bench but were refused permission. The following year Arbuthnot returned to the attack. Firstly, he dealt with the number of licensed houses in the town.

There is one to about every 151 of the inhabitants, or if you deduct the number of children of School age, there is one to every 120 persons over 14. Two evils result from this. First, people who cannot resist the temptation to take a glass, when they would be better without one, have their difficulties multiplied; and secondly, licence-holders are tempted to resort to illegal, or at least undesirable, methods to increase their business, since it is impossible that so many houses can flourish in such a comparatively small population.

He then took the Magistrates to task for not inspecting the licensed premises personally.

In years past it has been too much the custom to leave all such enquiry, and inspection to the Superintendent of Police. I maintain that however able and independent such an officer may be, it is throwing far too much responsibility upon him. The Magistrates are the responsible people, not the Police, who serve under their orders. . . . I do not wish to use too strong expressions, but I must say that last year's plan of granting or, to use a common though mistaken expression, renewing the licences, did not impress me as the best way possible. It was done 'en bloc'; some licence-holders merely sent the money; not one word of counsel or caution was administered; it was the most perfunctory job I ever saw. I trust we shall soon see an improvement.

He regretted that the Bench had taken no action about the undesirability of serving young children with intoxicants and finally wrote,

And perhaps it is asked – why am I writing thus in the magazine. It is because our Memorial was disregarded, and Mr Armistead and I were refused a hearing last year. Thus the only way in which I can let my views be known, as Vicar of the Parish, is by publishing them in this little sheet which is so largely read by my Parishioners. I trust I have written nothing disrespectful of the Bench, nor hostile to the licence-holders, the great majority of whom I feel sure are as opposed to drunkenness as I am myself.

In 1903 he was allowed to speak on behalf of the Ministers of the town. The police were also taken to task for terminology. He wrote:

> It is high time our Magistrates took notice of the perjury – we use the word advisedly – which is committed in cases of drunkenness brought before the bench. There has been some curious contradictory evidence in recent cases, and some which look very like wilful perjury. Is it not time too that it was settled what being drunk means? A man or woman is either drunk or sober – such expressions as 'having had a glass', and 'neither drunk nor sober', and 'not quite steady', ought not to be allowed in a court of justice. We have no desire to be unduly severe on a poor man who gives way to temptation, but we have every wish to see the sources of temptation diminished.

In another issue the following item was printed:

> We are inclined to offer a reward for the best description of the degree of drunkenness. The other day in our Police Court, a constable described two young men as 'the worse for beer, but not drunk'. Is this the comparative degree, and where-in does the worseness consist, if it has not made the man drunk? If the young men were sober it seems a libel to describe them as 'worse for beer', if they were not sober, surely they were drunk. Drunk, drunker, drunkest, sober, soberer, soberest. Bad for beer, worse for beer, worst for beer. Good with a little beer, better with less beer, best with no beer. We commend these degrees to the Chief Constable next time he examines a man for admission to the Police force.

Further opposition was made to the extension of licensing hours on occasions like the Queen's Diamond Jubilee. He felt particularly strongly that no licence should be granted to the Volunteer Camp in 1905. His sermon on the subject had given some offence. He felt he had been misquoted so he published it in the magazine. Here is part of it:

> Let me give you an instance, an unhappy instance of blindness or indifference to the spread of this sore. I speak with reserve because I know I cannot be answered here, were I on a public platform I should use much stronger language. Next Sunday there will be a camp in a field by our fair river not half a mile from the town. Thither on Saturday afternoon will congregate people from all the neighbourhood to see their soldier-friends. God's trees will wave beside them, God's grass will grow beneath them, God's water will flow past them. It will be a beautiful sight but, as in Eden, the serpent will be there. Last week an application for a licence to sell intoxicating drink there was made to our Magistrates, and they granted it by two to one. They could not indeed allow the drink to be sold on Sunday – I do not know that they would not if they could – but on Saturday from morning until ten o'clock at night – mark the hour – the curse of drink will be in that camp. I speak not of the soldiers, they are provided for, and rightly so, at their canteen, but I speak of the so-called weary thirsty visitor, who cannot, so these gentlemen think, walk out from Stratford and return without the use of alcohol. I cannot trust myself to say more than that I deeply regret that any of our Magistrates should be willing to play the part of Dives, and put temptation in such a way before their fellow countrymen.
>
> These were the actual words I used. I do not regret nor withdraw one of them,

and under similar circumstances I should pursue the same course again.

He was told that the matter had nothing to do with him and he replied:

> I claim the right as one to whom the Cure of Souls in the Parish has been committed, to refer to social and moral questions which affect the well being of the people in my charge. If public officers, as the Magistrates, act in a way which I consider unworthy of the high office they hold, I am justified in publicly expressing my regret.

He was very concerned about the effect of alcohol on work. In 1882 he quoted 'Two considerable employers of labour said that after Christmas men did no return to work because "they had been enjoying themselves" and if they did go to work they would be no use.'

He was even more concerned about the effect on working class pockets. In 1906 he published the following:

> But we call attention to the tremendous waste of money on intoxicating drink which was exhibited by the statements made at the adjourned sessions to consider the case of four houses reported for closing. According to statements made on oath these houses supplied a working class constituency, that is to say they did not cater for visitors, and their weekly takings averaged over £10. Now we have gone carefully through the list of licensed houses in the town, and we find that about 26 or 27 of them do the same kind of business. This means that the working classes in Stratford may be supposed to spend something like £260 or £270 a week in drink, or between £13,000 and £14,000 a year. We do not expect all to become teetotallers, but we must say that this expenditure is excessive, and we would ask the working men among our readers to consider whether it could not be reduced, with increased comfort to themselves, and increased happiness to their wives and children.

In 1907 for several months the magazine published cases of drunkenness which had been brought before the magistrates. Here is a selection.

DRINK REGISTER

(Continued from Last Month)

> Some misapprehension appears to exist as to the object of this register, which was started three months ago. We stated then, and we repeat now, that our intention is to rouse the conscience of the community by showing the inequality of the penalties inflicted in cases of drunkenness, and by calling attention to the fact that no prosecution is ever instituted against those who have supplied the drink. We do not wish to hold up the victims to opprobrium, and therefore in the case of all local residents we give the initials only.

> Wednesday, Sep. 25 – Before the Mayor and Mr Winter – *Ellen Poole* from Leamington, pleaded guilty to be helplessly drunk on the Birmingham road. She had eighteen pence on her, but on promising to leave the town she was discharged, having had a night's free lodging and her meals at the expense of the tax-payers.

> Thursday, Sep. 26 – Before the Mayor, Dr Nason, Dr Greene and Mr Everard –

J—P— for being drunk in West street was fined 5/- and 5/- costs, this being his second appearance in two months. W—B—, charged with being drunk in Henley street; had been able to run and so was discharged after a night's free lodging. A—I—, was drunk in Rother street, on Sep. 21st and was fined 2/6 with 2/6 costs. If we are not mistaken this was a third appearance which justifies his name being put on the Black List, unless the Act of Parliament is a dead letter.

Monday, Sept 30 – Before Dr Green and Mr Boyden – W—D—, helplessly drunk in Tyler street at 4 p.m. on Saturday. Had 13/- on him, of which he was mulcted 2/6, costs being remitted, it is difficult to see why. *John Allibone* of the Workhouse, charged with misbehaviour and using obscene language (but according to the Master's report to the Guardians very drunk), 21 days' hard labour.

Tuesday, Oct. 1 – Before Mr Winter – *Ada Palmer*, who left Shipston Workhouse the previous Friday to look for work was charged with being very drunk the previous night at 9 o'clock in Chapel street, pleaded guilty but was discharged, having had a night's lodging and meals at the tax payers' expense.

Oct. 24 – Before the Mayor, Dr Nason, Dr Green, Messrs Everard and Boyden – H—G—C—, described as mad drunk in the Birmingham road in the afternoon. Fined 2/6 and 2/6 costs. A—L— pleaded guilty to being drunk in Rother street 5/- and 5/- costs.

Oct. 25 – Before the Mayor and Mr Winter – *William Bardon*, drunk in Birmingham road 2/6 and 2/6 costs. Charge of assaulting the Police dismissed. 'Probably the man resented being interfered with,' said a Magistrate.

Oct. 31 – Before the Mayor, Messrs Smallwood, Boyden and Winter – F—S— drunk in Narrow lane at 11.45 p.m. 2/6 and 2/6 costs. Then followed this instructive conversation. A Magistrate: 'Cannot we find out who serve these people?' Superintendent: 'That is what I should like to know.' Magistrates Clerk: 'You can try, but there is no evidence in this case that he got drunk from a public house.'

Nov. 4 – Before Mr Winter – *John Harris* pleaded guilty to being drunk on the Shottery footpath at 9.25 p.m. Had 3/6 in his pocket. Used very bad language. 2/6 and 1/- costs so he had free lodgings for two nights and left the Court with 2*d*.

Nov. 7 – Before the Mayor, Dr Nason and Mr Everard – A—C—, drunk near the Fountain at 10 p.m. Two previous convictions within three months, 5/- and 14/6 costs. Is not this a case for the Black List? F—G—W— drunk on licensed premises, having been locked up for a night, was dismissed with a caution.

Nov. 18 – Before Mr Winter – *James Hyland*, described as quiet, civil and drunk, was fined 2/6 and 2/6 cost.

Here we end our sad list, which commenced on July 8th. We have shown that during less than 5 months 54 persons have been charged with being drunk, but not a single case has been brought against a drink seller, and a man who has been drunk, and violent, and used bad language has frequently been fined the same amount as a man without a lamp on a bicycle, or one whose chimney caught fire. Our readers can no longer plead ignorance of the extent of the evil.

He knew, however, that the real victory against drink rested with the individual and his philosophy was well summed up in this paragraph:

But the administration of the Licensing Act does not rest with the majority of those who read these lines. What they can do, and what I beg them to do, is this. They can be exceedingly careful in their own use of intoxicating drinks, never, for instance, drinking except at meals, never frequenting public houses; they can refuse to give drink to others as a sign of friendship, or a reward for services; and they can teach the young never to touch alcohol in any form. If they will only do this, regarding it as a duty they owe to their Church and Country, they will be doing their share in reforming the drinking habits of the people, and, by God's blessing, we shall yet be freed from the intolerable curse of drunkenness.

Chapter 13

WORK WITH YOUNG PEOPLE

In 1880, at the beginning of his incumbency, George Arbuthnot paid great attention to work among young people. He began with Sunday School; he was particularly concerned with the older scholars and wrote, 'The practice of leaving Sunday School when the day school is left is a bad one,' and he let it be known that he would not confirm anyone under the age of fourteen.

Other youth groups were nurtured. The choir boys were seen to be particularly important. He promoted the Band of Hope with genuine fervour. A Drum and Fife Band was formed by the latter which was encouraged to perform on every possible occasion. There was also a branch of the Girls' Friendly Society and later on, in 1904, a Church Lads' Brigade. The Vicar's field was the venue for cricket and football.

So, with choir practice, band practice, junior temperance, dancing and needlework classes, there was plenty for young people to do on week nights.

From the Parish Magazines a picture of healthy activity emerges with a strong sense of discipline. In 1883 he wrote, 'I wish it to be clearly understood that if parents send their children to Sunday School they are placed entirely under my control, and I punish them if necessary, as I think fit. On no other terms can I receive them.' Since there were eight hundred in the Sunday School at that time, most parents appeared to agree.

Very strong inducements for joining in any one, or several, of these activities were the treats and excursions which were earned by good attendance. Although the emphasis was on fun, there was often an educational bias. Mr Arbuthnot did not believe in wasting any opportunity to improve the mind.

The organization of some excursions was tremendous. On a visit to Ragley Hall, for example, six hundred were taken by train to Wexford and then walked the rest of the way. Breaks were ordered to carry the older teachers back to the station. Outings were arranged for as many as a thousand participants most years.

Summer Sunday School excursions for infants were held mostly in Stratford on the Vicarage lawn, but occasionally a field at Luddington or Shottery was used. The following is of such an outing on August 5th 1884.

> The children assembled at the Schools in Back Lane, and at Shottery, at two o'clock, and found six large wagons waiting to convey them to Luddington. They were soon mounted, and then a few teachers took their places in each wagon to keep order. Crack went the whips, round went the wheels and the party was off. Was there ever such a ride? The cheers resounded through the town, fathers and mothers

> rushed to their windows and frantically waved their handkerchiefs! Teachers forgot their responsibilities, and became children once more. Thus the journey was passed, and when Luddington was reached there were the kind host and hostess and their family, ready to welcome the visitors, and make everything pleasant. The beautiful meadow which borders on the river was soon well-filled with a laughing crowd of nearly 250 children, beside equally happy grown-up people. And in games and sports the afternoon sped away until tea time. Two by two the youngsters danced off to the barn, where a sumptuous repast was provided, only to be equalled by that afterwards given to the teachers, on the lawn. But at last came the hour for 'goodbye', and the wagons again received their loads, the horses were yoked, and all were ready to start. Then the Vicar called for three cheers for Mr and Mrs Wilson, another for the young ladies, and another for the young gentlemen, and right heartily they were given. If giving others pleasure gives happiness, the host and hostess, Miss Kendall and her teachers, were happy people that night. The return journey was as successful as the other, and soon after eight all the little ones were safely returned to their mothers' arms.

Quite often each child returned home clutching a bag of sweets, a bun, and toy. On one occasion on the Vicarage lawn, an Italian Organman who happene to be passing was invited in to provide music for the party.

Various local landowners within walking distance entertained the seniors fron time to time. The Phillips, and later the Trevelyans at Welcombe were frequen hosts. When funds were available part of the journey would be taken by train. I the 1900s Mr Holland's Recreation ground at Bidford became a popula destination, where a river trip down to Cleeve Mill was usually included.

At parks and fields, games were organized. At Kenilworth, Ragley and Warwic sightseeing tours were arranged for those who wished to see ruins and gardens The clergymen set up cricket and rounders matches for the boys while the girl played 'Kiss in the Ring' and other playground games. Some landowners provide swings and ropes for tug-of-war, and, inevitably, the 'Aunt Sally' was carried t the venue, to be used as a coconut shy. A regular feature was a scramble for sweets Then there were races, and afterwards prizes were awarded. Somehow it woul be discovered that every child had won a prize; tops, sweets, bags of marbles, an penknives were very popular gifts.

Sometimes Luddington, Shottery and St James' arranged their own 'treats' bu mostly everyone joined together. Because of smaller numbers, Band of Hope an Choir outings were more adventurous, and when these groups were included i adult excursions they had some long and memorable days. We read of a tri beginning at 5 a.m. which ended next day at 2 a.m.; one outing returned at 5 a.m from the Isle of Wight. On a choir outing to London in 1887 part of the day wa spent at the American Exhibition where Buffalo Bill very kindly admitted th 'boys free to the afternoon performance in consideration of their coming fron Shakespeare's town'.

London was a popular venue and as many sights as possible were crammed int each visit. After seeing such places as St Paul's, Westminster Abbey, Madan Tussaud's or the Zoological Gardens, the party would end the day at Earls Cour where everyone could enjoy the Great Wall and other attractions. Thes experiences must have enriched the lives of the boys and girls who had little opportunity for travel. Arbuthnot, defending expenditure on train fares, said that for many scholars it was their first journey by locomotive and of great educational value.

The following account of a choir outing on 11th August 1884 clearly shows a mixture of sober sightseeing and fun.

Choir Treat

The annual treat to members of the Choirs of the Parish Church and St James' took place on Monday, August 11th. A numerous party, amounting to about fifty, assembled at the Great Western Railway Station at seven a.m., and soon afterwards a start was made for Oxford, the place selected as the *locale* of the treat. The Choristers were accompanied by the Vicar, and the Revs E. J. Scarlett, G. H. Moor, W. R. Pughe, and H. F. Moor. Arriving at Oxford about nine o'clock the party proceeded to 'see the Lions' under the guidance of the Vicar, who most kindly and ably acted as a perambulating guide book. Visits were made to Christ Church, Magdalen, Keble, All Souls and other Colleges, the magnificent Chapel of Keble College being specially admired. An excellent dinner had been provided at the Clarendon Hotel, and ample justice was done to it by the hungry sightseers. After the dinner the bulk of the party enjoyed themselves by rowing on the river. One of the boats was a gigantic tub, and was dubbed by its occupants 'Noah's Ark'. We believe that the passengers and crew numbered over thirty! Some wonderful feats of oarsmanship were performed by senior and junior choristers, and if there was a lack of 'finish' about the performance there was plenty of energy – sometimes a superabundance, resulting in the occupants of the stern coming in for an unexpected shower bath. After a voyage of about three miles and a half, the 'Ark' safely reached Sandford, where the party disembarked and refreshed themselves with ginger beer, bathing, etc., returning to Oxford about six o'clock for tea at the Clarendon. The little time that remained after tea was spent in strolling about the City, inspecting the shops, and making purchases for friends at home. Leaving Oxford at 8.11 the party arrived safely at Stratford soon after ten o'clock having thoroughly enjoyed a most pleasant outing.

Most excursions were completed within a day but in 1885 the indefatigable Rev. H. F. Moor took fourteen of his senior Sunday School lads to Windsor accompanied by the Rev. J. J. Smith. They took a train to Oxford where they spent two hours looking round the Colleges. From Oxford they rowed to Abingdon for lunch, the Vicar having provided yet another hamper of food. They stayed the night at Wallingford, and rowed thirty-four miles to Marlow next day, where Mr Arbuthnot joined them. Windsor was reached by 2.30 p.m. on the third day, and after three hours sightseeing (including a flying visit to Eton) they arrived back in Stratford by train at 10.00 p.m.

When the Church Lads' Brigade was formed we read of Summer Camps in North Wales where there was much competition to be the smartest unit.

A lot of noise was made by excited participants. There were races on Meon Hill and the Malverns. There was a lot of singing on return journeys in railway carriages and breaks, and many loud cheers given for hosts and staff. Nevertheless discipline was maintained. The Vicar himself usually dealt with the group o hopefuls who had not been present at the required number of attendances t qualify for a 'treat', and who tagged on to the end of the procession hoping to 'ge away with it'. I don't think they ever did.

The usual way of getting to any place was on foot, so unless a child suffere from a real handicap everybody walked as a matter of course and an outing t Welcombe was not considered too far a distance for an afternoon out. Even whe a train was taken, there was often a fair distance to cover on foot, for example every one walked from Long Marston station to Meon Hill.

When Mrs Arbuthnot took her class of older girls to Malvern, or London breaks were ordered to carry them up the hills, or across the city. Ponies wer once hired at Malvern.

Various excursions took place by boat. Some were on professionally-ru steamers, like the one which took a party from Weston to Ilfracombe, and som were in rowing boats. In 1881, one hundred and sixty members of th Temperance Society and the Band of Hope rowed a fleet of small boats fro Clopton Bridge to Hatton Lock, where Mr Ledbrook lent his lawn for tea. I poured with rain all the way back, and the Rev. J. H. Beck fell in.

Trains were the means of travelling longer distances. Often a 'special' wa booked and once, when the regular service from Stratford missed the connectio at Leamington, a 'special' was provided, though we are told the party lost tw hours of their precious day in London.

Whatever means of transport was used to reach a destination, most excursion were accompanied by the Band of Hope Drum and Fife Band. One of their firs engagements in 1881 was to head the procession of five hundred and twenty-tw children with ninety adults on their way to Stratford station to board a 'special' t Warwick. They played 'The King of the Cannibal Islands'. Naturally they playe at the destination as well and, on their return, after leading the procession back t the town, they played 'God Save the Queen' before the party dispersed. Thi became a regular pattern. Banners were carried too. It was a good advertisemen of colour, fun and jollity to attract other youngsters to join.

Food played an important part. Phrases like 'lots of cake and bread and butter' 'first rate tea' and 'sumptuous repast' are frequently used. If caterers did not giv good service they received poor advertisement in the Parish Magazine. Th manager of the Coffee Palace was reminded that 'Sunday Scholars can put awa more than half-a-pound of cake'. On that occasion further supplies had to b fetched from Stratford before the teachers could have their tea. Food which ha been ordered from the Castle Inn at Kenilworth 'was the least successful part o the proceedings neither quality nor quantity reflecting much of the credit on th caterers'. The report makes a further comment on the 'coloured water describe as tea'. On a very hot day at Ragley Hall, although the food was good, insufficien tea to drink was provided, so tuppence a head was knocked off the bill. However on one occasion greed overtook good manners. Some youngsters filled thei pockets, and were made to disgorge.

The account of another Choir Treat on August 7th 1880 gives delightful hint of the provisions contained in the 'numerous hampers' supplied by M Arbuthnot.

The Choir Treat

The combined Choirs of the Parish Church and St James' enjoyed their annual excursion on Saturday, August the 7th. Nearly all the Members accepted the Vicar's invitation and met at the Vicarage about 9 o'clock. Stoneleigh Park had been selected as the place to go, Lord Leigh having kindly given the necessary permission. The party numbering about fifty accompanied by the Vicar, Mr Moor and Mr Beck, were conveyed in three large breaks. Had the weather been more propitious nothing would have marred the pleasure of the day, though as it was, all seemed to enjoy themselves. Arrived at Warwick, a halt was made that the interesting Castle might be seen. Nearly all the party were conducted over the apartments and grounds, and were much pleased with all they saw. Up to this time the weather, though dull, had been fair, but hardly had the last of the party left the Castle when it began to rain in real earnest, a good steady downpour, which lasted without stopping till 5 o'clock. However, nothing, not even the pouring rain, could damp the festive spirits of the Choristers, and though the remainder of the drive to Stoneleigh was performed under circumstances the reverse of cheerful, they arrived at the place selected for lunch in good spirits ready to do justice to the good things provided. Under some of the thickest trees the contents of the numerous hampers were spread out, and many a sturdy carver felt his arms ache, ere all cried 'hold, enough'. Yet even small boys' powers of eating toothsome Swiss Pastry and Jam Tarts must at last come to an end, and an adjournment was made to a neighbouring shed where the seniors smoked their pipes and the juveniles assisted digestion by making a noise. Soon after the weather cleared up a little and various games were indulged in. Space would fail us were we to narrate half the fun that took place, and half the jokes that were made – how even the Clerical members of the party were as merry as any and left their dignity at home – how all tried to promote good fellowship and festivity, and how one well-known total abstainer was found with a *Bottle of Beer* in his pocket. About 6 o'clock the rain again descended and so a start was made for Warwick, when a cup of tea was thoroughly enjoyed at 'The Bowling Green Hotel'. Half an hour was allowed after tea for a stroll about Warwick, which was taken advantage of by some of the Boys to purchase a few trifles in the way of provisions for the homeward journey, such as 'cold fried fish', 'cocoa-nuts', 'toffee', etc. We hope they agreed with the dinner. The return journey, enlivened by many a song, was enjoyed in spite of a cold wind and driving rain. We understand that Mr Moor did his best to keep the Boys in his break quiet, but from the noise which they made on entering the Town we fear he failed.

The Vicarage was reached at 10 o'clock, and amidst hearty cheers for the Vicar for his genial hospitality, the party dispersed. We must add that great regret was expressed that Mr Grundy and Mr Fortescue were not of the party – other engagements compelled them to refuse the Vicar's invitation.

Things did not always go smoothly. On a trip to Kenilworth an eight-years-old boy was lost. He was found by strangers as he walked along the Birmingham Road. They restored him safely to the party at the station. Two young men in the Bible Class failed to catch the 9.40 p.m. train back from London having missed their way on the Underground. They therefore also missed a ride back in the break which was waiting for the party at Warwick at 12.40 a.m. So, they had to walk and arrived back home at 5 a.m.

Two accidents happened at Welcombe on the same day; a little boy nearl drowned, and a little girl broke her leg and had to be brought back to the Infirmar in the Vicar's pony carriage. Behaviour was mostly good but at Malvern once, th Choir School was reprimanded, 'some forgot how ungentlemanly it is to tak advantage of confidence reposed in them to do what they dare not do when in th sight of their elders'.

Epidemics of measles and scarlet fever caused cancellations from time to time These illnesses meant that day schools and Sunday school had to be closed as well The weather played an important part; long walks under hot sun were tiring, bu cold, wet weather meant miserable picnics and ruined 'best frocks'.

All these activities had to be paid for. Although there was a Sunday Schoo Fund, 'treats' were often financed by subscription. Some were run ver economically, ladies would give the food and the party would be held on th Vicarage lawn or similar venue.

The Marchioness of Hertford regularly footed the bill for the Infants' treat a Luddington, while the Vicar himself provided hampers and entertained the me and boys of the choir to a meal on trips to London. Many well-wishers provide prizes. An Australian, who had been born in Stratford, sent a medal for the bo who made the highest score at cricket. The Rev. J. H. Beck (the curate who fel into the Avon on a Band of Hope trip) went as a missionary to India. One summe he sent back enough toys for all the infants in Shottery and for many seniors a well. Sometimes scholars were asked to pay but the sum was usually augmented In the early 1900s those who chose, could pay 1*s*. 4$^{1}/_{2}$*d*. (7p) to go to Bidford, bu an alternative 'free' treat was provided for those who could not or did not wish t pay.

The winter months saw many entertainments. The Drum and Fife Ban practised, Mrs Arbuthnot's girls' choir learnt their songs, and the Girls' Friendl Society prepared gifts for bazaars. Plays and recitations were given to boost fund for the many clubs. Christmas parties were arranged. Apart from the usual tea entertainment was provided by Magic Lantern, a conjuror, 'waxwork' tableaux o 'Punch and Judy'. Political Correctness was unheard of. The adventures of th first named gentleman with the baby and the hangman, leading as usual to roar of laughter.

This final account is of a Christmas Treat held on 29 December 1881. Eve today one can catch something of the splendour and excitement of the occasion.

The Sunday School

The Christmas Treat of this school deserves more than the short notice which we were able to give last month. The kindness and co-operation of so many friends in giving the children pleasure deserves to be recorded, and may we hope, may be taken as a happy augury for years to come. It was decided by the clergy and teachers in council, that the Treat this winter should take the form of a Christmas Tree; but that that decision, far from ending discussion, only in reality began it. Where was a tree big enough for 700 children to be found? And when found where was it to be erected? Then, how was it to be lighted? And from what mine of wealth was the money to be drawn to supply its rare fruit? These and similar questions were the cause of great anxiety, but were all at last satisfactorily solved. First of all, Mr Edgar Flower most kindly and generously presented a splendid Tree more than twenty feet high. Then it was found the Corn Exchange could be hired for a comparatively small sum, and Mr Latimer, in the most obliging way, made all the arrangements easy. This further facilitated the lighting of the Tree, for it was found that a large gas pipe was laid under the Exchange, with a special view to use at entertainments; and so it was determined to discard the traditional candle, and the tree was lighted with more than a hundred gas jets, with their pipes skilfully twisted among the branches. And finally the mine of wealth turned out to be in the kind hearts of many parishioners, some of whom sent money, and others gifts, for the adornment of the king of the forest.

At four o'clock the Tree was lighted for the children of the Infant School, and it was a pretty sight to see more than 250 little ones, under eight years of age, dancing merrily rounds its laden branches before they were presented with some of its fruit. The enjoyment of the little folk was further increased by the gift of a good substantial bun and an orange, from a box kindly given by Mrs E. Flower, while Mr Fortescue and Mr Beck warmed their inner man by a mug of hot tea or coffee from the adjacent Coffee Palace.

After the infants had been dismissed to bed and dreams of Fairyland, the more serious business of the evening commenced, in the Tea at the Schoolroom, to the Boys and Girls and the older Scholars from Shottery, numbering in all between four and five hundred. We do not know which was the pleasanter sight, the vigour with which the children attacked the cake and bread and butter, or the activity with which their kind Teachers sprang to serve them. We are sure both enjoyed their work, and we believe that such scenes as this must knit tighter the bond of affection which ought to exist between Teachers and Taught.

When Tea was over, the children had a short quarter of an hour in the playground while the Teachers partook of some light refreshment, and then all were marshalled in order, two deep, and marched down to the Corn Exchange. A few disappointed Scholars, whose marks alas did not entitle them to the Treat, caused some trouble by hanging on the outskirts of the company, but in consideration of their misfortunes, they were tenderly treated, and the one or two whom the Vicar caught were dismissed with a caution. At last the long line of Scholars safely reached the Hall, and, giving up their tickets as they entered, caught sight of such a Tree as none of them had ever seen. Its height nearly reached the ceiling, its branches literally beamed with light, and its rich green foliage was varied and enlivened by the lovely fruit which had been hung there, consisting of useful articles of clothing, bright sparkles and glittering reflectors, articles for the pocket, books and knives, articles for the home, paint boxes, and even scent bottles, articles for the playground, marbles and pistols and whips, articles for the throat, sugar plums and sweets of all descriptions. It was interesting to watch the way in which different children displayed their pleasure and astonishment, some indulging in loud exclamations, but the majority seeming lost in silent admiration. But then came the best part of the evening's entertainment, which consisted of giving away beautiful presents from the Tree, and from some tables which bore those which the branches could not sustain.

A pleasant surprise was arranged at this stage for the Vicar, who found amid the branches two parcels directed to him, and who, as no clue to the kind donors was given, asked us on his behalf to thank them very sincerely.

By half past ten all was nearly over, but it required a little gentle pressure to induce the last lingering spectators to disperse, and we doubt not many acted all they had seen and done over again in eager stories to friends at home, and bright dreams after they fell asleep.

We must conclude this rather lengthy report by saying that, from first to last, everything seemed to go off well, that the kind exertions of Teachers and Friends could not have been surpassed, and that the order and discipline of the Scholars, amid a scene of such unusual excitement, were deserving of the highest praise. We do not suppose that a Treat on such a magnificent scale can take place annually, but we think we can wish nothing better for the School than that, when its next Christmas Tree is grown, it may prove as successful as that of 1881.

All this energy was directed to providing social activities in decent surroundings where young people could find companionship.

Most of all, however, George Arbuthnot ardently wished that every child in Stratford should be taught the Christian faith within the framework of the Church of England, and to this end he worked tirelessly throughout his ministry of twenty-nine years.

Chapter 14

ENTERTAINMENT

It should be kept in mind that during the Vicar's time in Stratford almost all entertainment was 'home made'. The town was fortunate in having a theatre, though the Festival Season was short. The chief places of recreation were the public houses and George Arbuthnot, in his never-ending battle for temperance, worked hard to provide alternative places and methods for relaxation.

There was a great deal of potential talent on which to draw. Young ladies of good social standing and decent education learnt to play the piano or another instrument. Young men with reasonable voices would be prepared to give a solo. Choral singing was popular, and boys and girls were encouraged to recite their 'piece'. Some of these performances were of a high standard, but a good deal of tolerance was shown to those of lesser ability. Most entertainments were in one of two groups. Firstly, the weekly or fortnightly meetings of the many clubs and societies – Band of Hope, Mothers Union, Choristers, Bellringers, C.E.T.S., G.F.S. and others, where friends could meet regularly; and, secondly, the advertised events performed to raise funds for various Church activities. The latter were often prepared by the former. Thus the Choristers usually gave a Concert around Christmas time for their own benefit, and the Band of Hope, under the guidance of Mrs Arbuthnot, produced several operettas and 'Service of Songs' to raise funds. The G.F.S. and Mothers Union held working parties to produce goods to sell at bazaars, which was another convivial way of spending time with one's peers.

Lectures with lantern slides were popular. Sometimes these were given to clubs. The G.F.S. had one on Longfellow and another on 'Birds and their Habits and Homes'. Other lectures, on a variety of topics, were open to everyone. Canon Browne, of St Paul's Cathedral, spoke on 'St George', Canon Luckock on the 'Life and Times of John Wesley', and Mr Arthur Evans lectured on the 'Oberammergau Passion Play'. There were very many travel talks, some given by the Vicar himself and his assistants. After a lecture on 'The Giant's Causeway' was given by Reverend W. T. E. Carey at Luddington, it was reported, 'If all Clergymen who took holidays would bring back such interesting reminiscences with them, the people would be more willing to spare them, and both pleasure and profit would result to all.'

A debating society was promoted at the Men's Institute.

The division between entertainment and instruction can be very blurred. A course of lectures on the Prayer Book, or Church History, or preparation for Confirmation Classes, may not be amusing or relaxing, but such meetings must

The Firs

The Garden at The Firs

(Both photographs by permission of The Shakespeare Birthplace Trust, Stratford-upon-Avon.)

have been popular, and were further opportunities for meeting friends.

Indoor events took place in the National School Room, the Parish Hall, the Town Hall and the Corn Exchange. Occasionally the Memorial Lecture Room was used. Some smaller meetings were held in the Business Room at the Vicarage.

In 1897 the Vicar built the Parish Parlour, a large Iron Hall, in Evesham Place to commemorate the Queen's Diamond Jubilee. It opened on February 18th with a Public Tea at which the Lady Mayoress drank the first cup. The tea was followed by entertainment which included Vocal and Instrumental Music and a lecture by the Vicar on the Life of Shakespeare in Stratford, illustrated by limelight views.

The hall held 250 to 300 people for concerts, and tables could accommodate 160 for tea. There was a small room for groups of about 20 people. This could be hired for 1/- if no gas or attendant was required.

The large hall cost £1 if no more than a shilling was charged for the more expensive seats. If seat prices were raised the cost was raised to £1 10*s*. 0*d*. These costs were cut by 25% for all Parochial or religious Societies. When no heating was needed the charge was only 10/-. Crockery and tables could be hired at 1*d*. per head, and this included boiling water and services of a woman.

A harmonium was provided without charge, and a piano could be hired.

Food played an important part in most entertainment. Very special services in Church were often followed by tea or supper. At Shottery, after a Service of Dedication, 150 were present at a Feast where 'the utmost geniality and friendliness prevailed'. One popular method of catering was for a group of ladies to provide 'trays' of food, and each of the ladies would preside at a table.

Physical activity was promoted, particularly for boys. The Vicar's field was used for football, rounders, cricket, Church Lads' Brigade Drill, and School Sports Day. When the Church Institute opened there was a gymnasium, ping-pong, and rifle shooting. We are told of one cycling expedition by the girls led by Mrs Arbuthnot. Several rowing boat excursions are described with church members taking the oars.

In the Summer the Vicarage Lawn was a favourite meeting place. The G.F.S. and the Band of Hope held regular meetings there, while Bazaars, Sales of Work, Missionary Rallies and Garden Parties were annually hosted by the Vicar and his wife. Their tennis lawn was sometimes used for tournaments at fetes. At their invitation, any parishioner, applying for a ticket, could relax in the garden every Sunday afternoon. The garden was the venue for innumerable teas, including the Annual Tea Drinking of the Mothers' Union, and, probably the most important, the Celebration of the Festival of St James which developed into a jamboree of Church Services with processions, a good tea, and lots of homely fun.

Many of the Open Air meetings ended with dancing to the Drum and Fife Band or Mr Flower's Band. At Shottery, after a fete held in the grounds of the Hall, 'dancing on the Lawn was carried on to the tuneful strains of Mr A. Callaway's Band, and, as usual, large numbers displayed their Terpsichorean skill'. Another year, at Shottery Flower Show, there was dancing to the Band of the 2nd Volunteer Battalion, Royal Warwickshire Regiment.

The Vicar's nieces, the Misses Arbuthnot, were often involved with entertainments. Sometimes they aided their Aunt. We hear of Miss Muriel helping with a display of Pole, Flag and Garland Drill. They took part in plays, and on one

occasion were the object of some criticism when they performed 'Grass Widows
in the Memorial Lecture Room. The play was considered 'unsuitable', but th
Vicar thought it was harmless fun.

The Misses Arbuthnot also joined in many of the rather superio
entertainments promoted by Miss Hodgson. Miss Allfray and Miss Flower wer
other helpers. These shows were more sophisticated and required mucl
decoration of rooms and participants. On one occasion the Lower Room of th
Town Hall was transformed into a Drawing Room, as a setting for 'novel an
delightful' Tableaux Vivants. (For a Bazaar in 1889, the Town Hall was converte
into a ruined Abbey! But that event was not organised by Miss Hodgson.)

Other special efforts were Café Chantants, Costume Balls and Children'
Fancy Dress Balls, and they were treated as important social events. One Concer
given in aid of the Clothing Club Bonus Fund was described as 'quite a feature c
the Winter Season in our quiet town'. Unlike the entertainments at a more work
a-day level, the price of tickets for these is never given in the Parish Magazine.

There was an enormous range of diversions from which to choose, to sui
every taste, from Penny Readings to Cinderella Dances, from Communit
Singing to a Soiree Dansante (Mrs Laffan and Mrs Graves kindly giving thei
chaperonage). There were Firework Displays, Royal Handbell Ringers, Orga
Recitals, Industrial Exhibitions, Agricultural Shows, Waxworks, Sales of Work
demonstrations of drill, and operettas.

Concerts were probably the most popular form of amusement.

Very occasionally there were problems of behaviour. A concert at Shottery wa
marred by the noisy conduct of 'a few hobbledehoys who, we hope, will b
refused admission at any future entertainment'. Children, rushing round in th
twilight on the Vicarage lawn had caused some damage to flower beds, so it wa
requested that in future they should leave at 8.30 leaving the senior members t
dance. One unfortunate year, permission to have a dance on the lawn at St James
Annual Celebration was refused, because in the previous year several people ha
come for the dancing but had *not attended a Church service.*

Certainly, within the Parish, an enormous amount of thought and energy wen
into arranging such a wide variety of activities.

The Church did support other entertainment in the town as well. Bazaars hel
in aid of the Nursing Home were well advertised, and much support was given t
the Hospital Ball, except in years when it was held on a Friday – any Friday, no
just Good Friday, was a Special Day in the eyes of the Vicar.

Chapter 15

FINANCE

George Arbuthnot could have been content to carry out the legal requirements of his Parish, officiating at basic services, baptisms, marriages and funerals. However, as we have seen, for twenty-nine years he carried out a wide range of social enterprises as well as an extensive programme of restoration. He also took on extra staff to aid him in his endeavours. Money, therefore, was a constant worry. A generous man himself, he felt that his Parishioners should take their giving seriously. He was sympathetic to the very poor. 'If you have nothing to give,' he wrote, 'God knows your wants and will accept the wish that cannot be fulfilled.'

Holy Trinity and Shottery had wealthy congregations. At Luddington, deficits were often covered by donations from the Marquis of Hertford, the Vicar himself, and one or two other well-to-do members of the Church. St James', however, had a poor congregation, was not endowed, and the building, though it was only twenty years old, needed a great deal of renovation.

In 1903, the Vicar wrote to the congregation of St James' calling their earnest attention to the offertory:

> You have an excellent Organist, and a good Choir, the Church is well warmed and lighted, and it is kept nice and clean, but the money which is collected weekly is quite inadequate to meet the outlay involved, and unless there is a great improvement, the Churchwardens will have a heavy debt to announce at the Easter Vestry Meeting. The offertory rarely if ever reaches £2 a Sunday. One Sunday evening when I preached there lately, the number of silver coins contributed by the congregation was only 9, although there must have been 300 people in Church, and only one of the nine was over *6d.* – one shilling, 4 sixpences, and 4 threepennies – that was all. There was a large number of pence, and I believe the poorer members of the congregation do give according to their means, but I think the well-to-do hardly realise their duty in this respect. I hope they will receive this reminder of it in a friendly spirit, and that there may be such an improvement in the collections as may enable the Churchwardens to meet the expenses which the proper rendering of Public Worship make necessary.
>
> I am, dear Friends,
> Your affectionate Vicar,
> G. Arbuthnot.

In spite of this appeal, St James' Accounts for 1902–1903 showed a deficit of £16 15*s*. 3*d*.

This was by no means the only occasion when he analysed the collection. In 1881 he published this 'breakdown' of a 'special' collection. There had been approximately 420 people in the congregation.

	Unit Value	Modern decimal value (approximately)
6 sovereigns	£1	100p
6 half-sovereigns	10/-	50p
13 half-crowns	2/6	12.5p
19 florins	2/-	10p
110 shillings	1/-	5p
175 sixpences	6*d*	2.5p
17 groats	4*d*	2p
193 threepennies	3*d*	1.5p
468 pence	1*d*	0.5p
301 halfpence	$^{1}/_{2}$*d*	0.25p
6 farthings	$^{1}/_{4}$*d*	0.125p

He advocated regular giving rather than 'one off' contributions. He had tried to establish an 'envelope' system whereby a sum was set aside every week. He found this was used extensively in America when he visited the States, and also among Dissenters in England. He warmly recommended the scheme in Stratford, but it never became popular at that time.

It was a constant struggle for the Vicar to raise enough money to pay his curates. In 1894 he published this personal account when appealing for extra funds:

Income 1894

I venture to add a few words on a subject which may be considered personal, but a knowledge of which is, I think, desirable for the Parish at large. I am often met with the statement that this is a good living, when I speak of the duty of the laity to subscribe for the maintenance of the clergy. I think therefore that it is better that you should know that I do not receive £200 a year for my services after payment of the necessary out-goings. My income and the sources from which it is derived may be gathered from the following statement. Of course several of the items are subject to fluctuations, and I do not assert that the figures are exact. You must only regard it as a rough statement, but it is sufficiently accurate to give you a general idea of the value of this 'living'.

INCOME

	£	*s.*	*d.*
Stipend from Corporation under their Charter	262	0	0
Fees from Charity Trustees	7	7	0
Share of Church Visitors' Fund	130	0	0
Cemetery Fees	35	0	0
Surplice fees	26	0	0
Easter Offerings	25	0	0
Endowment from Ecclesiastical Commissioners	50	0	0

Endowment of of Shottery and Luddington	90	0	0
Rent of Glebe	52	0	0
Rent of Vicarage	60	0	0
	£737	7	0

OUTGOINGS

Curates' Stipends	520	0	0
Expenses of Choir	30	0	0
	£550	0	0

It will be noticed that I say nothing of all subscriptions to Schools and Charities, in which the Vicar is expected to set a good example, and the only curtailment of outgoings possible would be to reduce the money spent on the Choir, and consequently its efficiency. I do not think I am estimating my work too highly if I say I ought to have an income of £300 a year and a house. At all events the Parishioners ought not to refuse to help me, simply because my Father's generosity has left me sufficient to live upon, independently of my profession. Almost the whole of my private income is spent in the Town, and I have often felt it hard that my people do not help me, even to the extent of keeping one Curate. It is very unpleasant for me thus to lay bare my needs, but I feel it is right to do so, considering the wide-spread ignorance which prevails.

Annual Church accounts were always published.

Apart from the money needed to run the Churches, endless appeals were made for Home and Foreign Missions; the Sunday School – its work, annual treats and prizes; the Day School, likewise; the Curates Fund; the Choir Expenses Fund; the District Visitors' Benevolent Fund; the Temperance Movement Expenses; the Clothing Club Bonus; the Coal Club Bonus; Infirmary Sunday, and many more worthy causes. Subscription lists were frequently published, and it is possible to trace the generosity of certain families in Stratford. Very small contributions were recorded as well as lavish gifts.

Restoration at Holy Trinity, and building work at the other three Churches, necessitated further fund raising. Stratford and Shottery Day Schools also needed extensions. It was little wonder that finance was a perpetual worry to the Vicar. Somehow he managed to balance the books and always he led the way in personal giving.

Not only money was begged. There were also Harvest offerings, flowers for regular Church decoration, and goods for sales of work and bazaars, which helped to augment Church income. Expensive bequests, like stained-glass windows, and Church furniture, often in memory of loved ones, were gratefully accepted.

No collection was made to build a much-needed Church Hall. The Vicar built one for the use of the Parish at his own expense.

The Vicar had several well-publicised rows with the Town Council and the Tax authorities over money. He conducted his side of each argument with vigour, and published his opinions in the Magazine. In 1888 the Corporation wished him to pay for repairs to the Vicarage House. (This belonged to the Town, who were legally required to provide a suitable dwelling for the Vicar. Arbuthnot bought his own property, The Firs, to be his Vicarage, but leased out the house provided by the Corporation.) At the same time he was told that his stipend would be reduced by £50 – nearly a fifth of his income. His reply was as follows:

THE VICAR AND THE TOWN COUNCIL

Exception has been taken, in some quarters, to the words which we applied, last month, to the action of the majority of the Town Council towards the Vicar. We called it mean and unprincipled. We adhere to the terms, and believe the great majority of our Readers agree with us. That there may be no mistake about it, we briefly re-state the Vicar's case.

1. The questions of the repair to the Vicarage House, and of the Vicar's Stipend, are totally distinct, and unconnected with one another.
2. In declining to repair the Vicarage, the Vicar has been following the advice of the Bishop of the Diocese, from the very first. Considering that the present Vicar has only a temporary interest in the house, he would have done wrong to have disregarded the counsel of his Diocesan Bishop.
3. Both the Bishop and the Vicar have frequently professed their willingness to abide by the decision of any duly qualified Arbitrator, or the result of a friendly, and consequently, inexpensive law-suit.
4. As regards the Stipend. When the Vicar accepted the living, he was informed that the Corporation paid him £260 a year. Not a word was said of any possible reduction. Considering the outgoings of the post, this is not too much to pay.
5. The Council now allege that owing to diminished income from the College Estate, they are obliged to reduce this by £50 a year. Let them prove this by publishing in plain figures the Balance Sheet of the income of the Estate, showing that there really is a deficiency.
6. Then, let them make a reduction in salaries all round, in proportion to the diminution of income.

Unless they do this, it is evident that their action against the Vicar is either the result of personal feeling, or from a desire to compel him to act contrary to the Bishop's advice.

An agreement was reached. A grant was made towards repairing the house, and it would appear that the whole stipend was restored to him. Certainly, three years later he was quoting £260 as the amount which he received from the Corporation. That year, 1901, he returned from holiday, to find that some of his furniture had been seized in lieu of unpaid income tax. And again, he set out his reasons in the Parish Magazine.

THE VICAR'S TAXES

The Vicar had an unpleasant experience on his return from his holiday, as he found some of his furniture had been seized on account of his not paying his Income Tax. Refusal to pay a tax is an action which requires an explanation, and so we are asked to make a statement on the subject. The tax which the Vicar has refused to pay is that on the stipend of £260 which he receives from the Corporation under their Charter, and it amounts to £13. The circumstances are as follows: the assured income of this living, amounting to £260, is payable out of the Church lands handed over to the Corporation by King Edward VI. There are of course other sources of income, such as Queen Anne's Bounty, and the Ecclesiastical Commissioners, but income tax is deducted before their payments are made. When the Vicar first came a claim for income tax on the £260 was made, but he explained that he paid it all (and a good deal more) to Curates, whose employment was authorised by the Bishop's licence. This explanation was accepted and nothing more was said until about three years ago, when a new man was appointed collector of taxes at Leamington. This person, with the zeal of a new broom, declined to accept the Vicar's explanation and an appeal to the Commissioners was made. These gentlemen, in 1899, sitting under the Chairmanship of Mr Cove Jones, received the Vicar's explanation, and disallowed the Tax. It was therefore with great surprise that the Vicar found in 1900, that the collector was determined to re-open the question. He was again summoned before the Commissioners – Messrs Cove Jones, D. S. Gregg and S. Sanders – and although he shewed that the circumstances were unchanged, they reversed their previous decision and they sustained the imposition of the tax. The Vicar then told them he should not pay, and that the collector should get the money how he could. The Vicar's reasons for this were – 1st, that he believes a Clergyman is entitled to deduct necessary payment for Curates before his income is assessed. Otherwise, as the Curates pay income tax, it would be paid twice over. 2nd, that if he paid now, it would be an acknowledgement that he has been acting wrongly in the last twenty years. 3rd, that the Commissioners gave no reason for their extraordinary change of opinion. If they are right in 1900, they were wrong in 1899.

It would appear that a compromise was reached, since no further developments were reported.

Chapter 16

THE VICAR

Not only can the life of the Church and Parish be traced in the magazines, bu
much of the character of the Vicar is revealed.

George Arbuthnot was a man of deep faith. Worship was the most importan
part of his work and the crowning glory of Worship was the Eucharist. He was
'High Church' man and used a great deal of ritual in his services, particularly a
Holy Trinity.

He wrote, 'I am satisfied to go on with the orderly and dignified Cathedral-lik
Service which we have enjoyed here for so many years.' He liked to see properl
robed clergy and choir, and the use of correct liturgical colours throughout th
Church year. If a parishioner made a request, he would hear confession, and h
once said that he could see no reason why incense should not be used in Anglica
Churches – though he did not do so. However, he wished to accommodate a
shades of opinion in his Parish, and said, 'There is room in the Church for all th
three parties of High, Low and Broad, with all their sub-divisions, an
consequently there ought to be room in every Diocese for each of them. I an
thankful to say that this is the case in the Parish of Stratford, and I am pleased t
be able to number among my congregation those who would describe themselve
as Low Churchmen, or Broad Churchmen, as well as High Churchmen. May i
be always so!' On occasion, his practices were rather too 'High'.

In 1891 the Archbishop of Canterbury published some guidelines on the Ritua
of Communion, and the Vicar gave up the ceremonial mixing of the Chalice an
making the sign of the Cross in Giving the Blessing. He said, 'We should shov
our willingness to yield to authority when we are satisfied that that authority ha
the right to demand obedience.' He encouraged his congregation to kneel fo
prayers and make humble reverence to the Altar on entering and leaving Churc
– practices not always carried by the clergy.

He was very protective of the dignity of his position. In 1896 he was invited t
the Annual Mayor's Banquet in a private capacity. He felt he should be invited a
the Vicar of the Parish, so he refused the invitation. He said he had no quarre
with the Mayor, but since the Mayor had the right to ignore him, and throug
him, the National Church, so the Vicar had the right to stay away from the feast
The other clergy also 'courteously declined His Worship's invitation'.

After funeral services, coffins had to be carried about three-quarters of a mil
to the Evesham Road Cemetery. The Vicar and his staff were perfectly prepare
to walk with the procession, but, if a family hired a horse-drawn hearse, instead o
the hand-drawn bier, he announced that the clergy would take off their robes an

walk separately to the graveside. They were not prepared to walk like grooms at the horses' heads.

He was uncompromising in his opposition to divorce, and remarriage of divorced people in Church. He also disapproved of marriage in registry offices. He would refuse to receive a woman for Churching after the birth of her first child, if the baby was conceived out of wedlock. He regarded 'the Churching Service as a means of grace provided for those who have kept the moral laws. While the Church does not wish to treat harshly those who have failed in this respect, the whole tone of the Service implies that they have no right to its use.'

He frequently stated that he had a great deal of admiration for certain Dissenters. 'Many of them set excellent examples in their daily life and are true Christians at heart,' he said, 'and Church people should love them and pray for them, and in many respects copy their example. But it is ridiculous to pretend that there are no vital differences in religious matters between them and us.' He had little patience with anyone who could not see the differences. He was very cross indeed when the Board of Guardians at the Workhouse sent a boy in their care to an Orphanage where no Church teaching was allowed. The child had been baptised in Shottery Church, but unfortunately his parents died. When the Vicar protested that they would have wished their son to be brought up as an Anglican, he was called 'narrow-minded'. He commented bitterly, 'They have saved the rates the keep of this child, but they have done for a poor man's orphan, what no rich Churchman would allow in the case of his own child, and they have gone against the conscientious objections of all right-thinking ratepayers, whether Churchmen or Dissenters.'

The Board of Guardians was not pleased when he asked a candidate for the post of nurse at the Workhouse, whether she was a churchwoman. He felt she had no cause to be ashamed whether she was Anglican or dissenter. He was instrumental in refusing a teaching post at the Board School to a Unitarian.

He advised all Parishioners to avoid meetings of the Church Association. This was a Society which wished to get rid of High Church Practices. Many local supporters were Dissenters. Of a non-conformist clergyman who spoke at a meeting in Stratford, he wrote, 'I confess that I cannot see how my esteemed friend and parishioner, the Rev. F. Fry, finds it his duty to protest against the manner in which I administer the Chalice, considering that he never attends the Service of Holy Communion, and if he did, could not receive the chalice until he had been confirmed.'

He returned to the subject of behaviour on Sundays many times. Worship must take priority and substitutes for worship should not be supported. 'Sacred Song' Services were held at the Corn Exchange which he described as rather pleasant concerts. The Congregationalists tried a similar meeting on Sunday afternoons. The Vicar was troubled to hear that they were trying to enlarge the attendance by inviting women. He suggested that they might like to go to Mrs Arbuthnot's Bible Class instead.

Nevertheless, since Sunday was a day of relaxation, he earnestly tried to give good advice about recreation.

In 1889 Sunday Excursions to Stratford were introduced by the Sunday League, and the Vicar wrote the following letter to his Parishioners:

Dear Brethren,

Many things are combining just now to make the question of Sunday Observances one of general interest to the community, and believing as I do that the Cure of souls in this Parish is committed to me by the will of God, and the Order of the Church, I ask your permission to write a few words about it.

I have never regretted having been brought up in what would nowadays be reckoned strict Sabbatarian principles. I believe that the better way of observing Sunday is to make it differ in very many points from all other days. The novel unopened, the secular newspaper unread, the business letter unanswered, these, in my opinion, all minister to a happy Sunday. But I acknowledge that even religious people are now more lax in the observance of the day, than was the case when I was young. We are indeed still far from a 'Continental Sunday', and I hope we shall always be, but things are done now, which, though not wrong in themselves, used not to be done on Sundays a few years ago.

I am often asked questions as to Boating on Sunday, Bicycling on Sunday, and other recreations of that nature, and it seems to me impossible to lay down a hard and fast rule about them. Are they right, or are they wrong? I can only say, I cannot answer.

But I think I can give you advice by which you should be able, each one for himself, to answer those questions, although it is possible that your answer may differ.

Sunday is the Lord's Day. Therefore the Lord has first claim on your time. The devotion of some of your time to Him is a debt, which it would be dishonest to refuse to pay. The best – though not the only – way of giving time to God is by attendance at Public worship. Attendance then at Church or chapel is the primary duty of all Christians on Sunday. I should go further and say attendance at the one Service instituted by Christ, that is Holy Communion, but I will not press that point because I want to carry you all with me.

Attendance at public worship – I will not say more – is our manifest duty on the Lord's Day.

When this is recognised, I believe the Lord allows us to spend the rest of His day in innocent recreation, subject to two conditions. First, we must not needlessly interfere with the rest and recreation of others, nor should we deprive brute animals of their day of rest. Secondly we must not offend, or put a stumbling-block in the way of those persons who perhaps do not see the question exactly in the same way as ourselves.

Sunday is the Lord's Day. The Lord has a claim on our worship. We are not alone in the world. Our neighbours – I use the word in its Bible sense – have a claim on our consideration.

In conclusion, I ask you to face the question. Don't shirk it, but make up your mind upon it. I have tried to write plainly and concisely. Give my words fair thought. And may God help you to decide what is right!

Your faithful Friend and Vicar,

GEORGE ARBUTHNOT.

Mostly, the Vicar had good relationships with the Nonconformist Churches in the town. On one or two occasions he invited their clergy to Services in Holy

Trinity. Several were present when the East Window was dedicated, and at the special service to mark the Coronation of Edward VII. It was reported:

> A pleasing feature of the Service was the presence of the Rev. W. M. Armistead, and the Rev T. B. Angold, Wesleyan Ministers, who at the Vicar's invitation occupied seats in a line with the Choir. The other Nonconformist ministers were invited, but from one cause or another were unable to be present.

He was genuinely appreciative of their support of the Temperance Movement and in the early 1900s many combined rallies were held.

He did not think very highly of the Salvation Army. In 1888 he wrote:

> Of the Salvationists I have only to say that, while I believe they are well-meaning, they are Dissenters just as much as, say, any of the other religious bodies who do not belong to the Church. The proper course, then, for Churchmen to pursue is to leave them alone. They go their way, and we go ours. The roads may conduct to the same end; but they do not touch or even run parallel, and it is impossible to travel on both. Churchpeople cannot be Salvationists; and Salvationists are certainly not Churchpeople.

He was concerned about the 'forward manner of young women who parade the streets in curious costume' and 'the impropriety of women conducting public services'.

He was also annoyed one Sunday morning when the Band could be clearly heard during a Service which was taking place in Holy Trinity. He did, however, admire their zeal and their fund-raising through self-denial.

He was never afraid to criticise those in authority. He complained about sewage in Shottery Brook, and the conditions in the slaughter houses behind the butchers' shops. He regularly upbraided the Town Council for owning Public Houses in the town, and was very concerned about the conditions of some properties which they owned. He suggested that the Mayor should visit Pinfold Court, Russell Court and Pimms Court, three very run-down areas, to see the conditions for himself.

If he considered that an Act of Parliament was applicable to a local situation, he passed on the information to the Parish, so he pointed out that the law limiting the working time of dressmakers' apprentices to sixty hours a week, applied to small shops as well as to factories.

He regularly published the sentences given to those found guilty of drunkenness by the local Magistrates Court. He always named the sitting magistrates, and questioned why the landlords who had supplied the liquor should not be prosecuted, too.

The Vicar's views on Temperance must have made for very uneasy relations with the Flower Family, the owners of the highly successful Brewery in Stratford. They were really generous and major employers of the Town. Financially, the family supported the Church well, giving much money and entertaining Church parties in their homes. Mr A. Flower ran a Bible Class on Sunday afternoons at St James', and Mr Flower's Quadrille Band played for many a Church function. Mr Edgar Flower had a house at Broadway where he welcomed excursions of choirboys, Mrs Arbuthnot's girls class, and even members of the Band of Hope.

When he died the Vicar made arrangements for a special service.

> A Memorial Service, Contemporary with the funeral of the late Mr Edgar Flower at Broadway, was held in the Parish Church on Saturday August 1st. Mr Flower had so endeared himself to his friends and his employees in Stratford, comparatively few of whom could travel to Broadway, that the Vicar felt it right to give them the opportunity of joining in prayer on the solemn occasion, and the attendance fully justified the action.

The death of another member of the family was marked with particular sorrow by the Vicar, that of Lieut. Richard Fordham Flower, who was killed in action in the Boer War. He was a very well-known and popular young man in the town. Arbuthnot said, 'There is not an inhabitant who does not feel that he has suffered a personal loss in his death.'

Arbuthnot's relations with C. E. Flower were not so convivial. There seems to have been some bad feeling between them right at the beginning of the Vicar's incumbency. When the scheme for the first stage of restoration of Holy Trinity was put forward at a distinguished gathering at the Town Hall, it was C. E. Flower who, before the main proposals could be made, proposed a motion that the meeting should be adjourned to that day three months. This was carried, and was the cause of a humiliating setback for the Vicar.

Another occasion when their differences were aired publicly occurred in 1888 when the Vicar was prepared to stand for election to the County Council. This article was published in the magazine and shows not only the rivalry between the two men but Arbuthnot's wish that working men and women should be represented on the Council.

> **THE COUNTY COUNCIL**
>
> Most of our Readers know that the new Local Government Act comes into force next spring. As its name denotes, its object is to introduce the principle of representative government into the management of local affairs. The business of County Councils as originally designed was much more extensive than is expressed in the present Bill; but there can be no doubt that subsequent acts or Orders in Council will largely increase this. It seems certain that the questions of Local Option, and Sunday closing of Public Houses, will have to be settled by the Councils; and most probable that the work of School Boards will eventually be handed over to them, as even now they are to pay for the schooling of the Workhouse Children. It seems therefore desirable that men, and women too (for we hope to see ladies on the Councils), should be elected who will rightly represent the views of the majority of the ratepayers. In all parts of the County large landowners, and wealthy men seem to be standing as Candidates; but we hope to hear of some Working Men Candidates as well. Stratford only returns one Member, but there is no appearance of a contest for the seat, and Mr C. E. Flower will have a walkover. The Vicar at one time intended to be a Candidate but has withdrawn. The history of his Candidature is this. It was stated in the *Herald* that bad health would prevent Mr Flower standing, and absence from England prevented Sir A. Hodgson. Next to those gentlemen, the Vicar is one of the largest ratepayers in the Parish, and moreover is well acquainted

with all classes of the community. He received a letter from the Bishop from which we are allowed to make the following extract: 'I do not see any reason why clergymen should not act on the new County Councils. It has been always the custom for them to act as County Magistrates, and in some cases I think that such action has been very useful.' Accordingly on November 12th he issued his Address to the electors, under the impression that there was no chance of Mr Flower standing. In this he was mistaken, for on the 14th appeared an Address from that gentleman declaring himself a Candidate. The Vicar at once decided that he could not in the interests of the Parish carry on a contest with Mr Flower; their views have already been too often brought in conflict, and nothing could justify an action which would stir up bitter feelings in many minds. And so, long before the so-called Requisition to Mr Flower was published – curiously enough *after* his Address – he wrote the letter which appeared in the *Herald*, withdrawing from the Contest. This then is how the matter stands. The Vicar will not oppose Mr Flower, but hopes on some future occasion to obtain a seat on the Council.

Whatever his differences of opinion with the Vicar, C. E. Flower was a very generous benefactor to the Church and the Vicar always acknowledged this.

Arbuthnot seems to have had an appreciation of beautiful things – a taste which extended to the Church building. He saw no reason why places of worship should not be made beautiful. He loved music and laid great importance to the use of the organ and choir in services. Concerts and singsongs were regular forms of entertainment and most outdoor events on the Vicarage lawn ended with dancing to a local band, though on one occasion a passing organ-grinder was invited to provide the music!

The Vicar was not a snob. He mixed freely with all his parishioners, and every Sunday afternoon in Summer he opened his garden to anyone who cared to share his pleasure. He had hoped that other members of the congregation would also create opportunities for fellow church-goers to meet together, since he was distressed that class-distinction should be present in the Church.

When a particular scheme failed in 1898, he wrote the following:

The Vicar's proposals about Social evenings to which we alluded in June, have not been developed, because no one has taken them up. Stratford Churchpeople who kneel together in Church do not 'know' each other when they meet outside, because they do not happen to move in the same social circle. These social distinctions are not only un-Christian, but they are a sad source of weakness in the Church. There are many hesitating between Chapel and Church who might be won to the Church if a little cordiality was displayed towards them by Churchpeople. We are better off here than in many places because we have free seats in Church, and any worshipper can sit where he likes, but we want further a welcome, and sometimes a hand-shake to the new comer, if our numbers are to increase. Then in Church-work the same difficulty presents itself. All Church-workers ought to feel that they stand on a common platform, and are engaged in a common cause. Let those who are in the higher ranks of society remember that they lose nothing by courtesy, and those who are not, be sure that working for their common Mother makes all equal. So let the Church gradually absorb the lower ranks of Society, who are one in Christ.

George Arbuthnot had a good reputation as a preacher and was invited to speak from many prestigious pulpits including Canterbury, St Paul's, Lichfield, Winchester, Worcester and Edinburgh Cathedrals as well as several London Churches. Once, he was asked to give the addresses during the three hour Good Friday Service in Worcester Cathedral, and he preached at Devonport Parish Church on the Sunday after the launch of H.M. Battleship Edward VII.

In return, many distinguished clergy came to preach in Holy Trinity.

We have already seen that he was a passionate believer in education. At different times he served on the boards of five local schools, and deplored the legislation through which local supervision was being superceded by officials who did not live in the town. He was always looking for ways to interest and stimulate young people in both mental and physical activities, being a firm advocate of a healthy mind in a healthy body.

He deplored the Warwickshire dialect, knowing that poor speech is a handicap to ambition, and he certainly believed in ambition. At a Prize Day at the National School, he spoke of the opportunity for a boy to win a scholarship to the Grammar School and, from there, to gain a further scholarship to University. He only wished that a similar avenue was open for girls.

He had a dry sense of humour and would, on occasion, tell a joke against himself or, at least, allow it to be reported in the magazine. On one occasion a letter to the *Herald* was quoted, 'If a petition for the abolition of the Vicar was sent round Stratford, it would get more signatures than one for the rustication of the Mop.'

Another anonymous correspondent, to the same paper, on the subject of the Vicar's return from America, wrote that it was a pity he came back.

When the Vicar of Ullenhall declared himself offended by Arbuthnot, the Vicar apologised, but added, 'It does not do for a Vicar to be too thin-skinned. We knew one Vicar . . . who may in fact be regarded as thoroughly pachydermatous, by a steady perseverance in reading the Stratford *Herald*.'

He was a very practical man. If there was a problem, he tried to find a solution. Although he was an abstainer, he could well understand the attraction of warm, friendly public houses to men whose homes were poor, miserable and overcrowded, so much alternative entertainment was arranged and a coffee house was opened.

Boys were full of energy and up to mischief with nothing to do, so the Vicar's field was constantly used for football and cricket. Later, he was able to equip a gymnasium in the Church Institute in Tyler Street.

The Mop Fair had a reputation for drunkenness and lewd shows, so a Temperance Bar was opened, and the upper classes of the town were urged to attend. Gentlemen were particularly asked to patronize the Peep shows and report any indecency to the Mayor.

He was very tenacious. Once he had decided on a particular course he used every argument to promote his point of view. Some crusades were successful. He achieved the abolishment of pew rentals after six years campaigning. It also took many years, and a great amount of personal persuasion, to get a half-day closing day in the town for shop workers – he was indeed still advocating an 8 p.m. closing time on Saturday evenings, when he left Stratford.

Some social problems were not solved. He tried many experiments to channel the energies of young men into worthwhile activities. After a period of popularity, each in turn lost its attraction, but he never gave up and always tried another scheme. His last projects in the Parish were the Lads' Brigade, and the Church Institute. His crusades to inculcate thrift and temperance received many setbacks, but he never gave up his efforts to encourage both.

Arbuthnot was a man of principle. To resign from the Hospital Management Committee because Charitable Balls were held on Friday nights may seem trivial to us now, but he held the view that all Fridays are sacred, not just Good Friday. He continued to act as Chaplain. When it became apparent that many people were enjoying the social activites on the Feast of St James, but neglecting the Church Services, he acted decisively, as the following letter shows:

Letter to Mr Wilson.

S. James 1898

I have long entertained the fear that the separation of our religious from our secular observance of S. James' Day might lead to the neglect of the former, and the very meagre congregation at the Services last night showed me that my fears are not groundless. I think we had better own at once that we have made a mistake, and determine for the future to return to the old plan, by which, after the Congregation had enjoyed a social Tea together, they went to Church to finish the day with praise to God. And for this year, the merry-making must be given up. I cannot bear to see numbers of young people dancing on my lawn in honour of S. James, who have ignored altogether the primary duty of praising God for his Saint.

I fear that this may distress you and the Churchwardens, but I am so thoroughly convinced that it is the right course, that I trust you will acquiesce, and, I hope that our present disappointment will lead people to see that the prosperity of a Church and Congregation must be built upon religious principles, and not on tea and cakes.

He was proud that he had been elected to be a Proctor in Convocation for the Diocese of Worcester, and he wrote a vivid account of the Special Service in St Paul's which was held entirely in Latin. He was appointed to the Committee of Elementary Education and the Committee on Temperance. When he did not approve of certain opinions agreed by the former, he wrote that he took early opportunity of disassociating himself from the conclusions of his colleagues.

George Arbuthnot's health was not always good. He seems to have suffered from some form of rheumatism for which he visited a number of spas in search of a cure. His voice, too, gave cause for concern, and sometimes he had to cut down on the number of services at which he officiated. Nevertheless, he was a very active man. He umpired and played cricket, and swam, cycled and played tennis, having a tennis lawn in the Vicarage garden. He also enjoyed fishing.

He drove a pony carriage and, on one occasion when a driver was indisposed, he drove a large carriage back from a Diocesan Temperance Fete, 'but his appeal to his load to "remember the coachman", was not properly responded to!'

He rowed. On one excursion by members of the Guild of the Holy Cross to Charlecote, he shared a boat with Mr Genge, the Curate. The Vicar took an oar part of the way, while Mr Genge 'acted the part of passenger to perfection' – even to the length of losing his hat!

He seems to have been an enthusiastic walker, both in country or town, enjoying excursions to the Malvern Hills, and acting as guide around Oxford and London. He not only enjoyed sport himself, but urged all young people to be active, and did his best to provide opportunities for their physical wellbeing.

On November 19th 1885, at the age of 39, George Arbuthnot got married. His eighteen year old bride was Margaret Evelyn Luckock, daughter of Canon Luckock, Principle of Ely Theological College, who in 1892 became Dean of Lichfield.

The family was already known to the Vicar. Canon Luckock had preached 'The Shakespeare Sermon' in 1884, and it had been published in the Magazine – a rather nice compliment to a future father-in-law!

The wedding took place in St Stephen's Church, South Kensington, and the honeymoon was spent in Italy where, unfortunately, the bride contracted typhoid fever, and an extra month had to be spent in Milan.

On their return to Stratford in 1886, they received many gifts from the Parish to mark the occasion. Within a month the young wife was undertaking public duties. She presented the prizes at the National Schools.* The Vicar spoke, stating what a pleasure it gave his wife to show her interest in the school by attending that afternoon. He seemed very proud of her. The Mother's Meeting gave her a framed photograph of Anne Hathaway's Cottage. He remarked, 'Such marks of good will give great pleasure to the Vicar and will always be carefully preserved by him,' and in a speech accepting another wedding present, he said, 'I hope and fully believe that the steps which I have taken in bringing a Mistress to the Vicarage, will add to the efficiency of the work which I am sent here to do.'

The first prize day was the forerunner of many such events, and she quickly became involved with Church activities. Her special interests were the Girls Section of the Band of Hope, the Girls' Friendly Society, and two of the Mothers' Groups. She was also a District Visitor, and gave a lot of support to the Abyssinian Mission. She was a gifted musician. She played the piano, the organ and the violin. She trained a girls' choir in the Band of Hope, which won several diocesan awards, and produced many musical entertainments. It is implied that a Masque, called 'The Circling Years', may have been written by her because it was announced in a magazine for 1889 that she had published the work complete with full stage directions.

She took her work with young people very seriously, and even sat voluntary examinations set by the Diocese and obtained very high marks.

She soon became a proficient public speaker, and gave lectures on subjects as diverse as 'Ely, the Camp of Refuge', 'A Canterbury Pilgrim', 'England over the Sea' and 'Heart of Empire', and often her talks were accompanied by Magic Lantern Slides.

She also sat on several committees, becoming local secretary of Waifs and Strays. She was also secretary for 'The Art and Industrial Exhibition' held in 1901,

* It was written of her in the school log book in 1889: 'Both teachers and children are very pleased to get a visit from her, as she always brings sunshine with her.'

and was responsible for much of the organization. Another of her projects was the Women's Fund for the Restoration of the Chancel.

Like many another Vicar's wife, she found herself in charge of Church decoration for all the major festivals, supervising the fetching of greenery from Welcombe at Christmas, and supplying nearly all the altar flowers from the Vicarage garden and greenhouses.

Although she was young, she must have learnt quickly how to cope with a staff of six at the Vicarage. She was a busy hostess providing trays for Church functions, cakes, bread and butter for Sunday School parties, and substantial fare for choir suppers. There must have been innumerable dinner parties for visiting clergy, along with other friends and relations as house guests.

The couple both received great help from their relations. George Arbuthnot's nieces joined in lots of entertainments, and Margaret's father came from Lichfield regularly to preach and give lectures. He and Margaret's sister took groups from Stratford for guided tours of the Cathedral and entertained them for tea. Twice, the Arbuthnots joined the Luckocks on holiday, once in the south of France, and again in Norway.

Twenty women attended her Sunday afternoon class, and fifty went to her Monday meetings. For those every year she organized outings as she did for her Band of Hope girls, the G.F.S. and her choir. These always appear to have been conducted with a certain decorum. Saloon coaches were booked on the railway, breaks were ordered to convey parties from St Paul's to Westminster Abbey. Return journeys from Broadway (by break) were planned when the moon was full and the night drive home was beguiled with song.

All the same, she enjoyed certain athletic activities. She and the Vicar were the first to reach the top of Bredon Hill on one excursion with a group of youngsters. She cycled, she may well have played tennis on the lawn of 'The Firs', and it is implied that she liked to swim. Her health did give cause for concern sometimes, and occasionally she had to go away for a rest. She was a generous woman, giving donations to many good causes under her own name, in addition to the contributions made by the Vicar. She gave prizes to the schools and Sunday Schools, and made several gifts to the Churches. In return, she received many tokens of appreciation from her groups, among them a tea service from her Sunday Afternoon Meeting, a silver mirror from the G.F.S., and silver topped bottles from the Communicants Union.

When she left Stratford, the Band of Hope gave her a picture of Holy Trinity and a bouquet. The Parish gave her a string (rope) of pearls.

George Arbuthnot's hope of giving an efficient helper to the Parish was certainly fulfilled.

George Arbuthnot's authority and personality make such a strong impression in the pages of the magazines, that it comes as rather a shock to realise that he was away from the Parish for at least four weeks each year.

He must have prepared for each absence with care, and many of his monthly letters were written in advance.

He obviously loved travel. He had been on a tour of the Holy Land in 1879, and was in Damascus when he received the offer of the living of Stratford. His wife shared his interest, and together they spent many holidays abroad in Italy,

France, Germany, Switzerland and Norway, as well as other excursions to Wales, Ireland, many parts of England and, most frequently, to Scotland where the Vicar was born.

Their most ambitious journey in 1894 was to sail to America on the SS Lucania, and travel right across the States to San Francisco. On longer holidays the Vicar sent letters for publication in the magazine describing their journeys. He had a lively and receptive mind, and described landscapes, cities, churches and occasions such as being present at a reception at the White House in Washington, where he shook hands with President Cleveland and his wife.

He was, of course, very impressed by the Temperance Movement in the States and, noting the antipathy between white and black races in the States, he wrote, 'It is to be hoped this will die out, as the coloured people seem to be every bit as good as the white, and some of them are now highly educated.'

He always described the Sunday Services he attended, commending certain practices and evaluating others. After visiting a church in Italy he said that he could see no reason why incense should not be used more widely. In San Diego, at a service on Christmas Day, he wrote of a female choir dressed in surplices, and wondered 'if we shall ever come to this in Stratford'.

He and his wife decorated their hotel room with cards and two photographs of Holy Trinity. Since there was no evening service they SAID Evensong together, and missed the Christmas bells.

In America he preached at Port Huron, returning the compliment to the Priest, John Munday, who had given a sermon in Stratford two years previously.

Several holidays were taken in an attempt to relieve his rheumatism. He tried the 'cure' at Salsomaggiore in Italy, but it did little good. He drank the waters at Strathpeffer several times, and in 1892 held a chaplaincy there for six weeks.

Church business, and preaching appointments, meant further absences from home and, when the Vicar became a member of Convocation, even longer periods.

In spite of so much continental, church and business travel, he still found time to take part in excursions with the Sunday School, the Band of Hope, the Choirs and various men's groups and to accompany his wife on many similar outings. Just as he wished to share his experiences abroad, he delighted in taking groups round Oxford Colleges, various Cathedrals, and acting as guide to the principle buildings of London.

He had some surprisingly 'modern' ideas. He supported Votes for Women (though he was not happy with some of the methods used by the Suffragettes), and he advocated university education for women.

He was outward looking in promoting many social activities, plays, dancing and mixed bathing, but he could also be prudish at times. 'Measure for Measure' was not a play fit for ladies, and he insisted that decency of dress should be observed at all sporting events.

He persistently extolled the virtues of cleanliness and neatness. Boys should be courteous and 'manly'. Girls should be modest and avoid cheap, flashy clothing and jewellery. If he disapproved of a fashion, he said so. Speaking to the G.F.S. on one occasion he told them that a women's most beautiful ornament is her hair which was so often spoilt by frizzing and fringing!

In spite of all the sermons and lectures, George and Margaret appear to have been very well liked. They were generous, hardworking and genuinely concerned for the welfare of their parishioners. The people, in their turn, reciprocated with many gifts and illuminated addresses to show their appreciation. When they left Stratford in 1908 they received innumerable presents and good wishes. The 'official' gifts, chosen by them, were the fees and robes for the DD Degree for the Vicar, and pearls for his wife. An album recording the names of all the subscribers was also presented. This pleased the Vicar enormously. 'With special gratification,' he noted, 'many joined in the gifts who have not been in the habit of worshipping with us, and we take this as an indication that differences of opinion need not interfere with personal friendship.' He added that he could not comply with the wishes of those present that he should put the robes on, as he had not yet written the compositions which would entitle him to take the degree!

George Arbuthnot became Archdeacon of Coventry, and went to live in Leamington. He died in 1922 and was brought back to Stratford to be buried in Evesham Road Cemetery. Twenty-nine years later, Margaret died in London, near the Church where they were married. She, too, came back here to be buried by her husband.